I'm Not Get for Kindergarten

Teachers don't have to cut out penguin beaks anymore. You can put your weather bear back in the cupboard (or bring it outside) and you can take the behavior chart off the wall. This book is your permission slip to break up with outdated and ineffective practices in your early childhood classroom and replace them with the magic of play-based learning! This helpful guide challenges outdated preschool practices in a kind and compelling way, inviting you to reflect on your own practices and adjust them based on current research and what is truly developmentally appropriate for young children. It provides tools and language to use to show the people outside your classroom (parents, administrators, other teachers down the hall) that play is learning. Each chapter is practical, comprehensive, and meant to be read in the order and at the pace that is best for you and your class. Full of stories from the author's own play journey, *I'm Not Getting Them Ready for Kindergarten* is key reading for early childhood educators who are ready to step outside the restrictions of an unnecessarily academic system and settle into the magic of play and child-led learning.

Kristen Day is the retired founder of a magical place called Butterfly Hill Nature Preschool. She is now a podcaster, international keynote speaker, and online entrepreneur, using her experience and B.A. in Education to help early childhood educators find play, settle in, and enjoy the journey.

I'm Not Getting Them Ready for Kindergarten

Breaking Tradition in Early Childhood Education

Kristen Day

Routledge
Taylor & Francis Group

NEW YORK AND LONDON

Designed cover image: © Kristen Day

First published 2025
by Routledge
605 Third Avenue, New York, NY 10158

and by Routledge
4 Park Square, Milton Park, Abingdon, Oxon, OX14 4RN

Routledge is an imprint of the Taylor & Francis Group, an informa business

© 2025 Taylor & Francis

The right of Kristen Day to be identified as author of this work has been asserted in accordance with sections 77 and 78 of the Copyright, Designs and Patents Act 1988.

ISBN: 9781032760292 (hbk)
ISBN: 9781032754147 (pbk)
ISBN: 9781003476719 (ebk)

DOI: 10.4324/9781003476719

Typeset in Palatino
by codeMantra

This book is dedicated to the four children who have inspired me to think differently about childhood and education: Sailor, Cru, Channing, and Knox.

You are my inspiration and my determination. Always stand up for what you believe in, fight for your rights and the rights of other people, challenge the status quo and live life unapologetically. And, please always be each other's biggest champion and supporter. I love you all.

Contents

Meet the Author

Kristen Day is a passionate and experienced play-based learning educator with a degree in early childhood and elementary education. Having founded and directed a play- and nature-based preschool in the Midwest, Kristen has established herself as a prominent advocate for play in early childhood education. Her dedication to the early childhood field is evident in her role as an entrepreneur, podcaster, and acclaimed keynote speaker.

Across various platforms such as podcasts, online summits, and speaking engagements, Kristen passionately encourages educators to embrace play-based methods. Her engaging presence extends to social media, where she shares laughter and insights with her followers.

Kristen resides on a lake in Minnesota with her four children. Apart from her professional endeavors, Kristen finds delight in exploring new places through travel, harbors a fascination with banana slugs and squirrels, and loves soaking up the summer sun on her paddleboard. Known for her lively spirit, Kristen firmly believes that kitchens are the perfect place for impromptu dance parties.

Introduction

Wow! I never imagined I would get the opportunity to share my experiences in a book. It is scary. What if I write something that I don't agree with in four years? What if I change my mind on something? What if someone reads this who has a bunch of letters behind their name and thinks I am off my rocker? What if? What if? What if?

Life is full of what ifs. But I have learned that the what ifs are what hold us back from moving forward. The what ifs keep us tethered to the past. They don't allow us to innovate. They keep us from being creative. The what ifs are keeping us small and not allowing us to grow and learn!

The what ifs is where people like to stay. If you haven't figured this out already, I have never spent a long time in my what ifs. I list all the what ifs, put on my cape and trust that, through my words, I may change the lives of one teacher or one child. If I can do that, I have done what I set out to accomplish.

I may not have 17 letters behind my name. I may not have a degree in play psychology. But I have had children wipe their boogers on my shirt and I've gotten barf in my hair. I have started my own play- and nature-based preschool. I have studied children every day for many years. And that, *that* makes me qualified to write this book.

If you have ever heard me keynote before, listened to my podcast ("The Play Based Learning Podcast"), or taken a training from me, you can probably already tell that I write just like I speak! You will hear my voice and my stories on every single

DOI: 10.4324/9781003476719-1

page. Even when I tell you all the brainy, researchy things, you will hear me in your ear.

I wrote this book for YOU. Yes, you. It could be for past you (you will find a lot of affirmation in these pages), it could be for present you (you might find some areas to reflect and grow), or it could be for future you (you may not be fully ready for the ideas in this book and could come back to it when your mind is ready)! Whichever *you* is reading this book, I am sure you'll see yourself reflected in these pages. You may see parallels to your own play-based learning journey. You may be challenged with new ideas that you never thought about before. Whichever YOU that is here, I am so thankful that you trust me enough to pick this book up and read it.

This book doesn't have to be read cover to cover. You can take what you need when you need it. It's like a choose-your-own-adventure book. And it really is an adventure. An adventure in becoming the teacher a child would choose. An adventure in becoming a play-based learning advocate. Or maybe even an adventure that is about to begin once you put the book down and decide to make incremental changes to better serve the children in your care. This book is not an end-all, be-all book for how to implement play into an early childhood environment. This book grew out of stories from my time in the classroom and I hope it will help others implement more play into their days with children.

Each chapter will start out with my own stories from my time in the classroom with young children. In those stories you may find yourself! After the stories will come some researchy and academia things for those of you who like the science or the brains behind the stories. Then I break into the "BUT Kristen" section. This section will answer questions I'm frequently asked about each topic presented!

Here are a few things I want to note before you race to the first chapter. First, all of the ideas in this book are my own twist on information and findings from all of the great minds that have come before me. I have many mentors that don't even know they've taken me on as a mentee. Some of those mentors are long gone and some are still alive and blazing trails. There are so many pioneers in the early childhood education industry, and my philosophies have grown from theirs. I have developed my own ideas and my own way of learning and interacting with children by drawing inspiration from the innovators who were doing this long before I came along. Lisa Murphy, Jeff A. Johnson, Bev Bos, Dr. Peter Gray, Dr. Stuart Brown, Heather Shumaker, Rae Pica, and Tiffany Pearsall (and every single child I have had the privilege to spend time with) have all greatly influenced my work with young children. I would not be in the position to write this book without the work each of them has done in the play and early childhood world!

Second, I use the terms teacher and caregiver interchangeably as we wear *both* hats in early childhood education!

Last, when using a child's name, every child will be called Lo in this book (for Little One) and the pronouns may be she/her, he/him, or they/them and may change for each story!

So here we go... buckle up. Books change lives and I hope this one changes yours in a positive way!

1

I'm Not Getting Them Ready for Kindergarten

Developmentally appropriate, play-based environments DO get children ready for Kindergarten!

My earliest memory of school was when I was in preschool at The Pumpkin Place. I don't remember much about The Pumpkin Place other than the tape cupboard. I remember the teacher opening the cupboard and searching for supplies. I would stand behind her and smell the yummy air that came out of the tape closet. It smelled like pencils, paper, tape, glue, and crayons.

I remember being in Kindergarten and realizing I could slice through a piece of paper with ease instead of opening and closing the scissors over and over. I frequented the library in elementary school and checked out books on craft projects so that I could "teach" my imaginary students that hung out in my basement playroom. I had a REAL desk and chair (you were legit if you had a real desk in your pretend classroom) and cupboards full of worksheets and craft supplies. I really leaned into the stereotypical teacher that stands in front and teaches everyone with a pointer stick. I handed out stickers and even timeouts for good and bad behavior to my stuffed animal and

DOI: 10.4324/9781003476719-2

doll students. I loved playing school and knew that someday I would be a teacher!

My elementary school BFF and I started a craft project club called "The Art Thing," and recruited neighborhood kids and my younger sister and her friends to sit and do craft projects. I was a little teacher and entrepreneur even back then! Our slogan was "The Art Thang Is the In Thang."

Fast forward and I graduated college with a Bachelor's degree in Elementary Education with a licensure in middle level social studies and early childhood education. I was living out my dream of being a teacher!

My early childhood education college classes included theory and practicums but there was not an emphasis on play or child-led learning. I learned that children learn through play when I started my first preschool teaching position. I was hired by a private preschool in my hometown and I dove in. I put on that teacher disguise and became the stereotypical eyes-on-me-one-two-three-criss-cross-applesauce-hands-in-your-lap teacher. I LOVED to plan for the weeks ahead and scour Pinterest for all the cute craft projects. I purchased a big old circle time calendar chart and felt I had finally arrived in the education world. The preschool's philosophy was that children learn through play. But, I hadn't ever defined what play is and I was under the impression that if something was fun, then it was play! If it was a game the children had to do, it was play! I felt the pressure of getting them ready for Kindergarten, so I did long circle times in order to get them ready to sit for longer periods of time. I did calendar time so that my kids would learn the days of the weeks and months of the year. I spent a whole weekend with a Cricut machine making adorable clothes for a weather bear so children could learn the weather. *Inside.*

Then my life changed. I went to an early childhood conference and listened to Lisa Murphy speak to my heart with her keynote. She changed my teaching career in that one hour. I did a deep dive, learning more about play, what play IS and what it ISN'T, and I realized that even though I worked in a preschool that described itself as play based, it wasn't true free play. It wasn't the type of play where children get into play flow. It wasn't the type of play where the learning sticks; the type of play that is about *true understanding*. I couldn't make the changes that I felt were necessary to be truly play based so I took a risk, quit, and made the decision to start my own preschool program. A preschool program where children are honored for the age they are and are allowed to *really* play.

In 2014 I founded a non-profit, play and nature preschool called Butterfly Hill Nature Preschool in central Minnesota. It was the first of its kind in our area. Butterfly Hill is a magical place and children are honored for the stage and age they are. They are given the MOST developmentally appropriate learning environment for three-, four-, and five-year-olds!

There are so many things that children are made to do in many preschool classrooms (in an effort to get them ready for Kindergarten) that are NOT developmentally appropriate AND steal play from three-, four-, and five-year-olds. I did *all* of them before I knew better. Worksheets, calendar time, criss-cross applesauce on the rug for long circle times, and teacher-directed craft projects with no process art in sight. After a lot of reflection and learning, I have concluded that early childhood educators do things that are not developmentally appropriate out of *fear*. Fear of what the parents/guardians will think when no ABC worksheets are sent home. Fear of what the program director or school administration will think when they don't see you making children sit at the table to do teacher-directed activities. Fear of what the Kindergarten teachers will think when children come to them. Fear of what the co-teacher or teacher down the hall will think if they walk past your classroom and see children "just playing."

My youngest two children were able to attend Butterfly Hill. I got to see each of them learn and grow through play.

When my son was three years old, he spent his time getting ready for Kindergarten by collecting toads in the forest. He couldn't contain them all in his hands so he did some problem solving and created little wrestling rings on the forest floor for the toads by brushing pine needles away to form barriers the tiny little toads couldn't easily hop over. He put two toads in his forest floor wrestling rings so he could facilitate a toad "fight" (they weren't actually fighting, just scrambling to get away). He had about 15 toad wrestling rings created when some other children came over to see what he was doing. They wanted to join in the fun. Soon, we had 30 wrestling rings with two toads each. The children started to chat about how many toads they had and started to count together to find out. They got lost in the numbers (it was about 60 toads!) and had to start over many times. They needed a bit of help from me as the counting got higher so I did some scaffolding and helped them out! Some of the older children decided they needed to sell tickets and popcorn for the wrestling match so they hunted down bits of nature to create these things. Bark with numbers etched on the underside became their currency and white flaky fungus from fallen logs became their popcorn. These children (my son included) had the magical opportunity to learn in all areas of development (social/emotional, cognitive, early literacy, and physical) through play!

When my son was four he got to spend his time getting ready for Kindergarten by coloring on his whole body with washable markers. He had never been one to pick up a writing utensil to make marks of any sort. He was much more interested in numbers and early math concepts than he was about making marks or learning letters. It was a summer day and I had just gotten back from a trip out west to visit a colleague and get some new tattoos. My son was fascinated by the tattoos and decided to give himself some new ink. Leg sleeves, arm sleeves, face tattoos—you name it, he colored it. He spent an hour covering his whole body in different colors. He used eye–hand coordination, fine motor skills; he crossed the midline, engaged in his own form of sensory play, developed self-concept, and practiced pre-writing skills! This is what whole child development is! Through play, my son was able to practice skills in all areas of development!

In our rush towards Kindergarten readiness, we often overlook the *profound* significance of play, Developmentally Appropriate Practices (DAP), and whole child development in early childhood education. It's *so* easy to get caught up in the check boxes of cognitive achievements: Can they recognize all the letters of the alphabet? Can they count to 20? By focusing solely on the

ABCs and 123s, we miss child-led learning moments, developmentally appropriate practice begins to slip and the whole child isn't developed. Just pieces. Why are developmentally appropriate practice, whole child learning and play so important to early childhood education? Let me explain.

Developmentally Appropriate Practice

Many educators have a hard time defining Developmentally Appropriate Practice (DAP). It is such a large framework that it is hard to boil it down to a succinct definition. The National Association for the Education of Young Children (NAEYC) offers a research-based framework that respects the individual needs, interests, and developmental pace of each child. DAP emphasizes understanding children's developmental stages and individual differences to create learning experiences that are appropriate and meaningful for each child. Kids love learning when the content is relevant and at their level, and they naturally create these learning opportunities for themselves when given the freedom. Early childhood educators who implement DAP principles recognize that children learn best when play and learning opportunities align with their developmental readiness, interests, and cultural backgrounds. DAP promotes individualized instruction, active engagement, and scaffolding to support children's growth and learning through play. There's no need to "sneak in learning" when the entire environment is engaging and relevant.

Whole Child Development

Whole child development considers the social, emotional, physical, creative, and cognitive development of children. I like to call this the Whole Child Pie. Each slice of the pie is just as important to the whole as every other slice! We can't leave out one domain of early learning to spend more time on another (which is often done in academic-focused early childhood environments). Whole child learning emphasizes nurturing all aspects of children's growth and well-being to support their overall development and learning!

Whole child learning is closely aligned with DAP and play-based learning, as it prioritizes the holistic needs of children and promotes a balanced, Whole Child Pie approach to education. Educators who prioritize whole child learning create inclusive, supportive environments that foster children's curiosity, emotional intelligence, social skills, cognitive growth, and physical health.

Fostering whole child development means creating an environment where children feel safe, respected, and valued; where their physical needs are met, and they are encouraged to express their emotions and thoughts. It's about supporting their curiosity, allowing them to explore their interests, and helping them to develop empathy and resilience so they can grow into well-rounded individuals!

Play

Have you ever seen puppies or kittens play? How about goats or panda bears? Play is essential for survival, well-being, and learning in mammals! Humans are no different. Oftentimes, adults believe that children should be allowed to play in school only *after* the work has been done. Play *is* the work of childhood and it is the most developmentally appropriate approach to early childhood education. Play *is* whole child development when there are supportive adults in the classroom who understand the nuances and importance of play in early childhood!

Play *is* the learning of children. It's through play that they learn about the world around them, themselves, and each other. Play is not just a way to keep children busy; it's how they process their experiences, experiment with the roles of the adult world, and develop critical social and cognitive skills.

Children learn by doing. Play is not frivolous; it is brain building. Play has both direct and indirect effects on brain structure and functioning. Play leads to changes at the molecular (epigenetic), cellular (neuronal connectivity), and behavioral levels (social-emotional and executive functioning skills) that promote learning and adaptive and/or prosocial behavior.

(Yogman et al., 2018)

Play has a significant role in children's development. Play is not just a fun activity; it actively contributes to brain development and enhances various skills essential for learning, social interactions, and emotional regulation. Understanding the profound impact of play on different levels of brain functioning can help parents, educators, and caregivers appreciate its value and prioritize playful experiences for children's holistic development.

Theory and research strongly support the benefits of play and since play provides children with opportunities to explore and interact with the world around them, it is not surprising there is a link between play experiences during early childhood and later school success.

(Fisher et al., 2011)

Through play, children learn to negotiate, cooperate, solve problems, and make decisions. They develop fine and gross motor skills, language skills, and creativity. They learn about boundaries, both physical and social. Play allows children to explore concepts of fairness, right and wrong, and the beauty and complexity of human relationships.

Researchers Rune Storli and Ellen Beate Hansen Sandseter studied 80 sessions of free play at 8 different early childhood programs in Norway. They found that children have better well-being during play compared with non-play, and children are significantly more involved in their learning during play vs. non-play activities.

In general, inviting play and providing physical indoor and outdoor environments that support a variety of play types in ECEC affords children opportunities to gain essential bodily, social, and cultural experiences.

As shown in this study, play is strongly related to children's well-being and involvement, and will as such be important to provide good psychosocial and learning environments.

(Storli & Sandseter, 2019)

When I first started to learn more about what play *is* and what play *isn't*, I came across the work of psychologist Dr. Peter Gray. I quickly learned that just because something is fun doesn't mean it is play! I thought that my Pinterest crafts and learning centers *were* play because they were either fun or a game! I added songs into calendar time so it was *fun*! Little did I know that all of my "fun" teacher-directed activities were actually stealing valuable learning from the children in my classroom! What I was planning and implementing in my classroom was the opposite of play according to Dr. Peter Gray's five characteristics of play (Gray, 2017).

Here is a very basic primer on the essential elements of play according to Dr. Peter Gray (2008):

1. **Play Is Self-chosen and Self-directed:** Play is an activity that children engage in voluntarily and is driven by their *own* interests and choices. It allows them the freedom to explore, experiment, and direct the activity according to their personal desires and curiosity.
    Example: A group of children decides to build a "fort" using cushions, blankets, and furniture. Each child contributes ideas on how to construct it and what it will be used for, such as a castle or a spaceship. There is no external direction given by the adults in the room; the children are making all the decisions themselves, from the construction to the purpose of their fort.

2. **Play Is Intrinsically Motivated:** Children engage in play for its own sake, rather than to achieve some external goal or reward. The joy and flow a child feels in play is the motivator and the learning that follows is the cherry on top!
    Example: A child spends a large amount of time gluing and glittering on a paper plate. They're not concerned

about showing it to anyone for approval or reward; instead, they're fully immersed in the joy of creation. The activity is driven purely by the child's own interest and pleasure.

3. **Play Is Guided by Mental Rules:** While play often appears unstructured, or maybe even wild and chaotic to the adult eye, it is governed by rules that are made up by the children's minds. These rules provide a framework within which children can explore, experiment, and engage in imaginative scenarios, helping to develop critical thinking and problem-solving skills!

   Example: During a game of "zoo," children assign roles to each other (zookeeper, cheetah, giraffe, wolf, etc.). They establish rules for their play scenario, like what animals get to have babies and when the zookeeper needs to feed the animals. These mental rules guide the flow and structure of their play.

4. **Play Is Imaginative:** Play often involves make-believe, imagination, or pretend scenarios (think back to playing when you were little)! Children are able to explore ideas that are beyond their reality, allowing them to flex their abstract thinking muscles!

   Example: Children playing "pirates" use a cardboard box as their ship, pool noodles as swords, and imagine an ocean in their play area. They navigate storms and search for treasure, fully engaged in their imaginative world!

5. **Play Is Focused on the Process Rather Than the Outcome:** The emphasis in play is on the activity itself rather than on achieving a specific end goal. This focus on the process encourages exploration and experimentation, allowing children to take risks and learn from their experiences without the pressure of achieving specific results! Afterall, the best learning happens through failure and trial and error!

   Example: Children playing with kinetic sand in the sensory table may build various structures like castles, roads, and mountains, without a clear plan or end goal. They modify and knock down structures, enjoying the tactile experience and the act of creation itself.

Children may create to understand an idea or theory, but they have the freedom or autonomy to investigate and change their methods as they make discoveries. Because learning takes place in autonomous environments, this work takes the form of play throughout the process.

(Hunter-Doniger, 2021)

Children use creation as a way to comprehend ideas when they're given the freedom to explore and modify their approaches as they uncover new information. This learning can only occur in environments where they have autonomy, and this creative work is expressed as play throughout the learning journey. Hands-on, self-directed learning isn't just a means to an end goal in preschool. It is the end goal!

How do integrating DAP, focusing on whole child development, and embracing the power of free play fit together and get children ready for the next stage in life? Each of these things in conjunction with each other does more than just prepare children for Kindergarten. They prepare children for life!

When I say "I'm not getting them ready for Kindergarten," what I really mean is that I'm preparing them for so much more. By valuing DAP, whole child development, and play, I'm respecting children's current stages, honoring their individuality, sparking curiosity, and nurturing their potential. And that, ultimately, is the best version of "getting them ready" I can offer.

I am NOT getting them ready for Kindergarten, because I AM getting them ready for Kindergarten, by letting them be three, four and five years old!

BUT Kristen, the parents/guardians want to see me teaching the ABCs and 123s…

If a pilot flew their airplane according to the passengers' opinion about the best course to get from point A to point B, I wouldn't fly on that plane. If an engineer built a bridge based on what the community thought looked nice, I wouldn't drive on that bridge. Yet, when I was in my teacher-directed teaching years, I let parent/guardian opinions guide what I expected children to do each day in my classroom! I was under the impression that parents/guardians expected craft projects each day and circle and calendar time. Now that I think back on it, did parents actually want that? Or was that my perception based on my own lived experiences and what I thought parents would want to see?

Early childhood educators are the experts in child development and early learning. It is time to take back our power and communicate to the adults outside the room that play is learning! We have to advocate for play by making learning visible to the adults outside the room. We can document learning by connecting play moments to the learning that is taking place in the domains of early learning. See Chapter 7 for more information on documenting learning.

In my experience at Butterfly Hill, parents were open to learning about play-based learning just as much as I was. The only reason they believed in worksheets is because that's what they did when they were preschoolers. Maya Angelou said, "Do the best you can until you know better. Then, when you know better, do better." When I showed parents the research behind our "why," they were on board. In fact, they became some of my biggest cheerleaders and play advocates! Parents want to give their kids the best start possible—they need us, as the experts, to show them what that is!

BUT Kristen, if I let children play, the admin/parents/guardians/ teachers down the hall will think I am not doing my job…

This is another place where we need to advocate for children. Now that there are many preschool classrooms in public schools, principals and other administration have likely not had a lot of experience or education about early childhood education. They were thrown into being a principal for preschoolers and they may be under the impression that a watered down version of Kindergarten curriculum is sufficient. They have not done the learning around play and early childhood, DAP, or whole child learning that we have. We have to advocate for play, DAP, and whole child learning by taking the time to teach others and by making learning visible through documentation!

BUT Kristen, I feel like everything I went to school for is a waste!

Not at all! First off, you've got a fire to inspire preschoolers, and that's irreplaceable. As I mentioned in Peter Gray's play elements, play often looks chaotic to the untrained adult eye. That's not you! You view everything through your teacher lens, and this gives you a huge advantage when transitioning to a play-based learning environment. You already know WHAT skills preschoolers need to be developing during their time with you and WHY; you're just giving your students the power to control the HOW, WHERE, WHEN, and WITH WHOM.

References

Fisher, K., Hirsh-Pasek, K., Golinkoff, R. M., Singer, D. G., & Berk, L. (2011). Playing Around in School: Implications for Learning and Educational Policy. In A. D. Pellegrini (Ed.), *The Oxford Handbook of the Development of Play* (pp. 341–360). Oxford University Press.

Gray, P. (2008, November 17). The Value of Play I: The Definition of Play Gives Insights. *Psychology Today.* https://www.psychologytoday.com/us/blog/freedom-learn/200811/the-value-play-i-the-definition-play-gives-insights

Gray, P. (2017). What Exactly Is Play, and Why Is It Such a Powerful Vehicle for Learning? *Top Language Disorders, 37*(3), 217–228.

Hunter-Doniger, T. (2021). Early Childhood STEAM Education: The Joy of Creativity, Autonomy, and Play. *Art Education, 74*(4), 22–27. https://doi.org/10.1080/00043125.2021.1905419

Storli, R., & Sandseter, E. B. S. (2019). Children's Play, Well-Being and Involvement: How Children Play Indoors and Outdoors in Norwegian Early Childhood Education and Care Institutions. *International Journal of Play, 8*(1), 65–78. https://doi.org/10.1080/21594937.2019.1580338

Yogman, M., Garner, A., Hutchinson, J., Hirsh-Pasek, K., Golinkoff, R. M., & COMMITTEE ON PSYCHOSOCIAL ASPECTS OF CHILD AND FAMILY HEALTH; COUNCIL ON COMMUNICATIONS AND MEDIA. (2018). The Power of Play: A Pediatric Role in Enhancing Development in Young Children. *Pediatrics, 142*(3), e20182058. https://doi.org/10.1542/peds.2018-2058

2

That's Not a Turkey

Child-led learning is a catalyst for wonder and discovery!

By now you will have figured out that I was the tried and true, criss-cross-applesauce-eyes-on-me-one-two-three-hands-in-your-lap-marshmallow-in-your-mouth preschool teacher. What I haven't told you is that I did in-home child care for ten months. Yep, I only made it ten months. It was the hardest ten months of my life (I bow down to all of you family child care providers). The one thing that I did LOVE to do was get my monthly themed curriculum kit in the mail from a well-known curriculum supplier. We did a lot of jelly bean things in April, farm animals in May, pumpkins in October, and the good ol' turkey in November. The kit came with all the craft materials needed for my two-year-olds to create a super cute turkey handprint craft (let's be real, I created it for them). It brought me so much joy opening that box and seeing the lesson plans inside. And the smells of the box! You know I love a good book-and-supply aroma. It was glorious because the turkey beaks were already cut out and I didn't have to do anything to prep ahead of time.

When I got a job teaching preschool I had SO. MUCH. FUN scouring Pinterest for themed activities. We had theme boxes in the back storage room packed full with materials from 30 years ago. The teaching team would get together to plan out the

DOI: 10.4324/9781003476719-3

themes for each week based on what was in the storage boxes and what had been done for the previous 30 years. The children were with us for 2.5 hours each day and we plannnnnnned that day. Every second was accounted for and there was very little room for outdoor play or free play. The free play that we did have was about 20 minutes long. Meanwhile, I pulled children (from play) to do craft projects or learning games with me at the table during that time. The rest of the day was filled with "table time," "center time," calendar/circle time, and, dare I say it, "school time." What is the difference between each of these? When it comes down to it, they were all the same. It was me standing or sitting in front of the children "teaching" at them or directing activities that children HAD to do. We did games and activities that I thought were fun (so that must be play, right?).

I remember leaving each day completely exhausted from the rush to get it all in. And thinking back on it, I bet the children were exhausted as well.

During Teddy Bear Week, I planned a craft project that ended up taking the whole week for children to complete (with a TON of help from the adults in the room). It was a larger-than-life construction paper teddy bear, and we used brads to make the arms and legs moveable. I am sure there are still a few of those out there in kids' memory boxes somewhere. But little do the parents/guardians know, I made most of it. I have zero fond memories from that crafting experience. I am sure the children felt the same.

During Thanksgiving I wanted the children to make the traditional handprint turkeys! They were going to be SO cute! I called each child over, sat them down, had them hold their hand out, and I painted their hand yellow, red, blue, green, orange, and brown. I guided their hand onto the paper and then they were free to go wash their hand at the sink. The next day I called them over to glue on an eye and a beak that I had already cut out for them. One child asked, "What is that?" when they saw their finished turkey. I told them it was a turkey for Thanksgiving. They said, "Our turkey doesn't look like that! Ours is meat. We eat it. It doesn't have any colors like that." That was one of the biggest "aha" moments in my early learning career. A child *usually* doesn't care about turkeys at Thanksgiving. And even if they did care, those handprint turkeys looked nothing like the real thing! I scrapped all the turkey themed things from there on out. UNTIL…

One day (I just fast forwarded about six years), when I was out in the woods with a group of children at forest school, we saw a flock of wild turkeys walking up a hiking path. Because the children were curious about turkeys after seeing the giant flock, we followed them up the path. The children noticed their footprints in the snow and got down low to take a better look. The language they were using was so rich and curious! "I wonder why they have a toe that goes backward?" and "I can't tell which direction they are going by these footprints." "This turkey has BIG feet!" "Do they have toenails?" "What do turkeys eat?" "Look, this must be turkey poop!" To extend the interest and learning later in the day, we dug out a turkey wing we had in the back room and some turkey feathers for children to explore. There were a couple of children who took a pair of scissors to the turkey wing the next day. They worked together to cut all the feathers along each of the feather quills. They collected the feather dust in a small bowl and when they were done, they had a turkey wing that looked like an Edward Scissorhands prop!

THIS. This is what child-centered learning is all about. Observing what children are curious about and finding ways to extend that learning and inquiry! The children learned about REAL turkeys that day and had first-hand experience seeing those turkeys out in the wild! And guess what? I have never had a child ask me to help them make a handprint turkey craft in all the years since I scrapped it!

Themes may be fun for *you* to plan. Themes may help give you a sense of organization, or you may be doing themes because that is what has always been done in early childhood. Not all children care about turkeys at Thanksgiving, or farm animals in the spring, or community helpers in the fall. And when children don't care or aren't curious about something, they don't learn it.

Many times, when adults hear the words "child centered" or "child led," they think the classroom will be taken over by a pack of feral cats. In her book, *Lisa Murphy on Being Child-Centered*,

Murphy says, "being child-centered is not chaos. It is not a room filled with screaming children throwing blocks at each other .... It *is* about children being able to investigate, play and explore within a space set up by adults who pay attention to children's needs and interests."

Child-centered learning places the child at the center of each day in the classroom (adult egos checked at the door). It recognizes that each child is unique, with their own interests, abilities, backgrounds, and learning styles. In child-centered learning environments, the curriculum should be flexible and adaptable to meet the individual needs of each child (hello emergent curriculum—more on that in a bit). Teachers act as facilitators, guiding children in their learning journeys rather than dictating what, how, and when they should learn.

Child-centered learning lends itself naturally to an emergent curriculum. The research suggests that teachers should move to an emergent curriculum because it allows for a more participatory and negotiated approach to learning (Sampson & McLean, 2021). Emergent curriculum encourages teachers to challenge their assumptions, let go of predetermined rules, and follow the thinking, questions, and interests of the children. By embracing emergent curriculum, teachers can create an environment that values children's thinking, embraces cultural differences, fosters deeper engagement, and supports their individual learning journeys!

So what is an emergent curriculum *really*? It can be such a buzz word so here is a basic breakdown of the characteristics of an emergent curriculum (and hint, it doesn't come packaged up pretty in a box or curriculum book!)

As adults, we may have realized that concepts we are not interested in don't stick in our brains, but information we value does! The same is true for young children! "Teachers who fail to capitalize on children's learning gained in informal settings would therefore appear to ignore a rich source of children's prior knowledge, experience, and interests" (Hedges, Cullen, & Jordan, 2011).

Emergent curriculum is a responsive approach to planning and implementing curriculum based on the interests, questions, and experiences of the children in the classroom. Rather than predetermining a set curriculum (like themes or boxed curriculums), teachers observe and listen to the children to identify their interests and then design learning experiences and activities around those interests. Emergent curriculum is dynamic and evolves over time as new interests and ideas emerge from the children's experiences and interactions. It encourages active engagement and meaningful learning experiences that are relevant to the children.

> Simply stated, emergent curriculum is an open-ended style of teaching and learning (Wien, 2008). It is not as simple in practice, however, and moving from a more traditional theme-based and adult-directed curriculum approach to understanding and implementing emergent curriculum can be difficult for some. According to Nxumalo, Vintimilla, and Nelson (2018), "emergent curriculum stands in contrast to, and is an important site of resistance to standardized and theme-based curriculum in early childhood education, including increasingly regimented modes of governing what children can do and learn in the classroom" (p. 434). Therefore, emergent curriculum is in opposition to adult-directed curriculum in early childhood education.
>
> (Sampson & McLean, 2021)

Emergent curriculum is all about ditching the old-school, one-size-fits-all teaching style. It's opening the door to a more creative, personalized learning journey for kids. Instead of rigid themes and strict rules, it's about following their interests and sparking curiosity. It's a game-changer in early childhood education, making learning more fun and meaningful!

> Rather than attending to the implementation of a given curriculum, research suggests that it is more effective to have a well-trained workforce, familiar with child development and the subject material, that recognizes and respond to the dynamic and individual nature of development in the early years and that can work with

an emerging curriculum that is driven by the interests and experiences of the children and the opportunities afforded by the environment.

(Hayes, 2008)

This is likely not the way you were taught to teach. It'll take some getting used to, but I don't want you to sell yourself short. You already have the foundational understanding of child development and the benchmarks of learning for early childhood. Hayes suggests teachers use that training in a new way! Now, instead of a dictator who directs all classroom activities in an exhausting choreographed schedule, you are a gold digger (not the booger picking kind), sifting through the child-initiated activities to find all the learning gold that's already happening!

People love to have control (adults and children alike). When things feel unpredictable, our stress levels go up. In a desperate effort to maintain that predictability, adults often think they need to control the little people in the classroom. Being child centered means that the adults have left their own egos at the door (Murphy, 2020) and are truly there for the children and their developmental needs. We have all heard the phrase, "The children in my class need more structure!" I would argue that, if adults say this, they actually mean "I need to control the children and the classroom." Murphy points out that "child centered spaces are structured, what they are not is *controlling*." Alfie Kohn (1993) writes, "when people talk about the need to control children, they very often mean that children cannot be left entirely to their own devices …. But to say that children need structure or guidance is very different from saying they have to be controlled."

Let's chat about adult control for a bit. The traditional image of a teacher is one that stands in front of children sitting in rows or a circle. This teacher verbally vomits information all over the children hoping some of it will stick (we will dive into this more in Chapter 4). However, we know that when children are able to make their own decisions about how they spend their time (cough, cough, when children are in control and not the adults), they are happier, which leads to less time spent on managing undesirable behaviors. Emergent curriculum, child-led learning, and play are their own forms of behavior management!

> This approach is intrinsically motivating to students, requiring less behavior management. Students make choices, decisions, and work as team members. Alternatively, a teacher in a traditional curriculum setting provides direct instruction and expends significant energy controlling student behavior. Students follow directions, recall previous knowledge, and work individually.
>
> (Zhbanova et al., 2010)

I witnessed this when I was teaching at Butterfly Hill in a fully play-based, child-led environment! I realized that when children can make the choices about who they spend their time with, how they spend their time, and the materials they choose, many behavior issues disappear. However, there will still be conflict and emotions when children are at play. This is part of working with young children—taking on the role of what I call a social-emotional coach. A large part of our job as play facilitators is to help children work through social conflicts and managing high emotions! When we are in the criss-cross-applesauce-eyes-on-me-one-two-three-hands-in-your-lap-marshmallow-in-your-mouth preschool teacher mindset, we forget that a LARGE chunk of DAP is social and emotional learning! It is part of the learning to walk through these things with children. The goal should not be to eliminate it completely and keep children busy with directed activities; the goal should be to give children time to problem solve with one another. And even though that can be uncomfortable or frustrating for the adults in the room, it is a huge part of the work we do with young children!

BUT Kristen, I love to have themes each week in my classroom. How does this fit into child-centered learning?
YOU love themes. Do the children really love the themes? Sure, maybe sometimes when there is a really exciting play provocation in the room for farm week. But farm items can be out anytime! Themes fit into a child-centered environment when

the children bring their prior knowledge and experiences into the classroom. Themes flow naturally when the adult in the room can observe and listen to the children in play. What are they curious about? What are they spending a lot of time on? What imaginative games do they enjoy playing? What are they asking questions about? Paying attention to these questions gives us ideas about what themes children are interested in. Your classroom can, and likely will, have learning themes; they just pop up more organically. They may only last an hour or they could last three weeks! That's the fun in child-led learning!

BUT Kristen, I have to do lesson plans each week for the director to check over. How do I possibly plan ahead if I am being child-centered?

At Butterfly Hill, instead of planning all of the teacher-directed activities, lessons, and learning centers (we didn't have designated times for those things), we planned out the environment and what we were going to place in the children's environment. We had a planning template that included each of the tables/areas in the classroom. We were flexible and added or changed things up based on the children and their needs and curiosities! Seek approval from the higher-ups to use this method for planning. If they need benchmarks/standards attached so they can see what you are hopeful children will learn, ask if you can submit the documentation of the learning after the week is over!

BUT Kristen, it keeps me organized to have a theme each week and I have boxes of themes in the backroom that I like to use with fun learning materials in them. Can I still use this stuff?

Let's back it up here a bit. Who are the themes for? You? Or the children? The answer should be child centered. However, you can ABSOLUTELY still use these things! I would suggest that you place the materials in the children's environment as a curiosity-inducer, also called a provocation or an invitation. Plop the things down and walk away. Resist the temptation to "teach" the children how to use the materials. See what they do with them. If there is something that requires specific instructions or safety protocols for use, introduce it in your morning check-in (see Chapter 11 "BUT Kristen" sections).

BUT Kristen, how do I communicate our learning plan to parents?
In a child-centered classroom, oftentimes things come up throughout the day. Themes emerge organically on their own and the "plan" can be diverted quickly! I liked to send home a weekly newsletter or email describing the learning that took place AFTER the fact. Traditionally, many teachers send home a calendar that describes what will take place in the coming weeks but who says that is what works best? We can change the script and send home a communication after the learning has happened! This is also where observation and documentation are essential in play-based programs (more on that in Chapter 7).

References

Hayes, N. (2008). Teaching Matters in Early Educational Practice: The Case for a Nurturing Pedagogy. *Early Education & Development*, *19*(3), 430–440. https://doi.org/10.1080/10409280802065395

Hedges, H., Cullen, J., & Jordan, B. (2011). Early Years Curriculum: Funds of Knowledge as a Conceptual Framework for Children's Interests. *Journal of Curriculum Studies*, *43*(2), 185–205.

Kohn, A. (1993). *Punished by Rewards: The Trouble with Gold Stars, Incentive Plans, A's, Praise, and Other Bribes*. Houghton Mifflin.

Murphy, L. (2020). *Lisa Murphy on Being Child Centered*. Redleaf Press.

Sampson, M., & McLean, C. (2021). Shifting from a Rules-Based Culture to a Negotiated One in Emergent Curriculum. *Journal of Childhood Studies*, *46*(1), 34–50.

Zhbanova, K., Rule, A., Montgomery, S., & Nielsen, L. (2010). Defining the Difference: Comparing Integrated and Traditional Single-Subject Lessons. *Early Childhood Education Journal*, *38*(4), 251–258. https://doi.org/10.1007/s10643-010-0405-1

3

Creativity Vampires

Child-led and play-based learning are the ultimate creativity muses!

Giant Squid Takeover

Lo came into the classroom one morning and announced he was going to make a giant squid. I asked him what he needed to get started and he told me lots of red paper and tape. We walked to the tape/paper cupboard together (oh the smells!) and I pulled out a brand new stack of red construction paper and a roll of masking tape and handed them over. His eyes got so wide and said, "I get all of this paper?" I said, "Well you are making a giant squid so I just assumed you need a lot of orange paper?" He smiled wide, turned, and headed straight for the art area. He set up shop on the floor in preparation for this massive undertaking. I went about my morning welcoming children into the classroom.

A little while later Lo came up to me and asked if we had something to measure the squid tentacles with. He told me he was making a male squid and the tentacles need to be 32 feet long. We walked to the janitor closet together and found a tape measure. I rolled it out to show him what the numbers mean and how to read the tape measure. I taught him how to push the button down so the tape measure would stay out. He rolled

DOI: 10.4324/9781003476719-4

that thing out to 32 feet and got to work. He cut and taped and cut and taped and cut and taped. He worked all morning on his giant squid. Other children were intrigued with his work (as tentacles and squid legs were now wrapped all around the classroom floor) and started wondering about what he was making. Lo knew quite a bit about giant squids and was able to teach the other children a bunch of giant squid facts. Sidenote: Did you know that giant squid have BEAKS? What sort of bananas creature lives in the ocean and has an actual beak?

Needless to say, the children were starting to be curious about these enormous creatures and Lo's creativity and knowledge sparked a very interesting day learning about deep sea creatures!

Now, if this was back in my "before I knew play" teaching years, Lo never would have had the opportunity to spend two hours on a creative project of his choosing. Nope! We would have had teacher-directed circle and calendar time, teacher-directed craft project time, and even teacher-led center time. Not only that, I would have been a creativity vampire by saying, "That is too much paper" or "Keep your art project on the table!" At what point would you have become a creativity vampire as Lo was creating his giant squid?

Pour, Pour, Pour Some More

During my traditional teaching days, I was the queen of the "Dot-Dot-Not-A-Lot" approach, scouring Pinterest for worksheets with small dots for glue practice. I thought teaching kids to say this phrase while gluing was genius, citing fine motor skills and self-regulation as key objectives in my lesson plans.

However, during crafting activities, I became the "GLUE police," constantly reminding children to use minimal glue. I'd say things like, "That's too much!" or "Remember, dot-dot-not-a-lot!" Little did I realize, I stifled their creativity and did NOT teach them self-regulation one bit.

I finally made the reflective decision to release MY control over the learning happening and lean into the magic of learning through play. I realized that children can't learn the right amount of glue for a project if they have never used too much glue or too little glue. And this is when the magic happened.

During the early days of Butterfly Hill Nature Preschool, a young girl stood at the art table on a chilly Monday morning, vigorously squeezing white school glue onto a large paper plate. Because this was early on in my "YES days," I refrained from interrupting her, even though my instinct was to say she was using too much glue. But I held my tongue, and I am SO glad that I did. I stood to the side and observed her process, and what unfolded has stayed with me forever!

I watched her face turn red with effort as she struggled to squeeze out the glue. She tried different positions, using her chest and chin to steady the bottle, and eventually she placed the plate on the floor to achieve better control and stop the flow of glue down the front of her shirt. After a bit more time, she bent over and slid the plate just under the edge of a table on the floor. She squatted down and placed the glue bottle in between her chest and the edge of the table. Using her arms to pull the table into her chest and glue bottle, she was able to get the rest of the glue out of the bottle and onto the paper plate.

This experimentation led to a messy but creative art piece, complete with a red pony bead at its center. Despite its wetness, she eagerly left it on the drying rack until her mother's arrival. The next day, she checked on her "Glue Plate" anxiously, discovering it was still wet.

We left her wet glue plate on the drying rack until the end of the day when her mom picked her up. The next morning, she found it still wet and exclaimed her disappointment. Throughout the day, she and her friends checked on it repeatedly, sparking curiosity and discussions about glue drying time and properties.

The excitement around the glue plate continued for several days, involving the whole class and even parents. It became a central topic of conversation and exploration, fostering imaginative play scenarios and deepening children's understanding of materials and processes.

Finally, after a weekend, Lo walked into preschool, slid out the art drying tray, looked down, her eyes got wide and she yelled, "Teacher Honey, I think Glue Plate is DRYYYYYY!"

Everyone stopped what they were doing to gather around her and Glue Plate. She was carefully and gently running her fingers across the dry glue that was semi-transparent, the little red pony bead barely visible beneath what now looked like a frozen pond. Lo's eyes were wide and her smile grew when her friends asked to "pet" Glue Plate.

Now that Glue Plate was our class pet, everyone wanted a turn taking care of it and Glue Plate became a loose part in our classroom for a few days. It was used in all sorts of play scenarios. I saw children using small items as people and "ice skating" the items on Glue Plate. Glue Plate became a tablet to take orders on while children were playing "store" and it was a plate of pudding when children were playing with it in the kitchen.

Over the next few weeks, more Glue Plates were made, and the OG Glue Plate was taken home by Lo.

Our classroom community would NEVER have had this amazing learning experience had I been the glue police and said "Dot-Dot-Not-A-Lot" when Lo started squeezing. The learning that took place could never have happened on a dot-dot-not-a-lot worksheet. This is whole child and child-led learning at its finest. If we break down SOME of the learning that took place amongst the children in four areas of child development, you can see that children learn SO much more when their agenda, interests, and needs are honored.

Preschool teachers are often guided by their fear of mess. If you are truly in the business of doing what is developmentally appropriate with young children, you will understand that mess is an integral part of childhood and exploration and can use the mess as part of the learning process.

Here are a few things to try:

- ◆ Contain glue play to a small table just for those projects! The glue can build up if there isn't time to scrub it down. Call it the Glue Table and let children use glue as another sensory play material and art medium.
- ◆ Have the children use trays that can be washed to contain their glue projects. The children can leave their projects on the trays to dry.

- Involve children in cleaning up the sticky mess. Give them "teacher" sponges and spray bottles. Children love to help clean up when it is a novelty and involves adult tools.
- Cover the tables with newspaper or a reusable tablecloth that can easily be removed once the project play is done.
- Reflect on why YOU are uncomfortable with the mess. Once you can answer this question, you will be closer to letting go of being the glue police.
- Ensure the daily routine allows ample time for uninterrupted free play and exploration. When the adults in the room recognize that play is how young children learn, we can let go of direct instruction during play and support children in their child-led learning experiences.
- Have aprons or large overshirts available for children to wear when they are engaging in messy play and exploration so their clothes don't get sticky.

When I was making children make handprint turkeys and giant teddy bears with brads, I was being a creativity vampire. When I planned each and every minute of the day, I was being a creativity vampire. Creativity vampires are anyone (generally adults) who sucks creativity out of someone else by making them do activities that are not developmentally appropriate! Think long circle times, teacher-directed craft projects, the pizza parlor incident (see Chapter 9), calendar time, and rotating center time.

I came across a magnificent and eye-opening TED Talk a few years ago by Dr. George Land called "The Failure of Success" (Land, 2008). His claims will blow you away and change the way you approach teaching. Land states that he was hired by NASA to create a test to determine how creative the astronauts are so that they don't do a spacewalk and float away never to be seen again. They needed the MOST creative thinkers to do these jobs. Land and his wife Dr. Beth Jarmon created the astronaut creativity test. "This is a test for the ability to look at a problem and come up with new, different and innovative ideas." Only 2 percent of these smarty pants astronauts could pass.

Land and Jarmon weren't satisfied that their work was done and wanted to determine the origin of creativity. Are some people born with creativity and others not? Or is it learned? Does it come from our experiences in life? They wanted to see if children could pass the test, so they gathered 1,600 four- and five-year-olds to take the test. The results are astounding! Ninety-eight percent of four- to five-year-old children passed the test in the genius category of imagination (Land, 2008).

Land was astounded by these results and went on to explain the results of his longitudinal study. At ten years old, 30 percent of the children passed, at 15 years old only 12 percent passed. Sir Ken Robinson said, "I believe we don't grow into creativity, we grow out of it. Or, rather that we get educated out of it."

We are sucking the creativity right out of our children. Our current education system, heavily focused on adult direction and left-brain activities, tends to drain the natural creativity from our students. It places minimal emphasis on, and fails to celebrate their capacity for divergent thinking, which resides in the right side of the brain.

Want to know the kicker? At the time of writing this book in 2024, The World Economic Forum (2023) predicts creativity to be the number one job skill employers will be seeking!

A study was done in 2022 that looked at 166 early childhood teachers to explore the ways that teachers support young children's creativity through play. The study looked at different roles teachers can play and evaluated which roles resulted in more creativity.

> Another finding revealed that there was no statistically significant relationship between the director role and creativity-fostering behaviours. "In the structured and teacher-directed play situations, the teachers' dominant roles were reflected from how they decided children's roles and actions through non-negotiable instructions" (Utami, Fleer, and Li 2020, 12). When environments are completely constructed by teachers, research suggests that this will impede creativity (Fox and Schirrmacher 2014; Robinson and Aronica 2015; Starko 2005; Tegano, Moran III, and Sawyers 1991). This is because the teacher who assumes a director role plays a simple and repetitive

role (Enz and Christie 1993). This finding is consistent with previous studies.

(Tok, 2022)

When teachers step in, creativity is squashed. Full stop. Mic drop. Adults need to get their noses out of children's play so they can dive into their full creative ability!

Child-centered approaches to learning parallel real-world techniques used by artists, scientists, engineers, and mathematicians. Because no career choice or discipline is completely isolated or siloed, the interdependence among the STEAM subjects mirrors real-life scenarios. In essence, by providing a variety of possibilities in each learning experience, STEAM education can inspire a sense of joy, engagement, and eagerness to learn in students.

(Hunter-Doniger, 2021)

Children are curious creatures. They explore, question and wonder, and by doing so, they learn. For too many children, curiosity fades. Curiosity dimmed is a future denied. Our potential—emotional, social, and cognitive—is expressed through the quantity and quality of our experiences. And the less-curious child will make fewer friends, join fewer social groups, read less books and take fewer hikes. The less-curious child is harder to teach because he is harder to inspire, enthuse and motivate.

(Perry, 2001)

Isn't it interesting how we celebrate inventors and thinkers who push boundaries and do things differently? We're quick to praise folks like that in history books. They are society's movers and shakers! But why do we often teach kids to conform and memorize instead of nurturing their natural creativity from the get-go? It's like we're holding back the very thing that could make them the next big innovator. We're stealing their innate creativity and replacing it with rote memorization.

BUT Kristen, I am tied to a bunch of standards and I have to do direct instruction to get it all in.

As soon as a teacher can fully trust play, they can clearly see that most of the benchmarks/standards in any state or country can be met through observing children in play. "The most effective curricular approaches in early childhood are based on young children as active learners emphasizing play, exploration, and constructive learning more so than didactic, teacher-led passive learning experiences" (Minnesota Department of Education, 2006).

We can use the standards as a checklist from any state or country (some are more developmentally appropriate than others) to see that children are learning through play. Observe them counting to 14 as they play with little rubber ducks in the water table? Check off one-to-one correspondence, eye–hand coordination, and counting a set of items! When children are given TIME to play (most of the day in early childhood), the adults in the room have TIME to observe and extract the learning happening to make it visible to the higher-ups that are requiring it! You can read more about the process I used with my students in Chapter 7.

BUT Kristen, I am willing to make the changes in my classroom, but my co-teacher doesn't have this level of knowledge or willingness to reflect.

The unfortunate thing is that we can't make people change or make people want to change. One of the first things you can do, instead of trying to persuade someone, is try to understand. Develop trust with your co-teacher and that may help you understand the root of their resistance. People have to be willing to listen in order to change, and that takes trust.

Once you've worked to develop trust, you can "start in the corner," as the late Bev Bos used to say. Break the big changes you want to initiate down into smaller changes. Want to go full on process art but your co-teacher is clinging to crafts? Begin with a modest approach by incorporating a handful of items onto the table, allowing children the freedom to create as they wish. Maybe it's recycled paper the children can tear, glue sticks, and cardboard. Start small so they don't feel threatened, and then add a little more each week if things are going well!

People like evidence that the unknown will be ok. If someone has never experienced a fully play-based environment, they may be resistant because it feels like a loss of control. If you can document learning that is happening in the small places you make the changes (use a simple tracking method shared above!), and make it visible to the non-believer, over time they may come to see the benefits!

BUT Kristen, I love doing craft projects with the children. And they love it too!

Do they? Have you asked all the children required to do a replicated craft project if they love it? Or is it that they just don't have any other outlet for artistic expression so they settle for teacher-directed craft projects? Maybe they have never experienced the benefits and rich learning that process art experiences can offer!

As the teacher, your responsibility is to create a rich learning environment in which children may grow. Just because crafts are fun, it doesn't mean crafts are the most effective way to encourage creativity and innovation in the preschool classroom. What if kids could have fun making art AND develop their creativity simultaneously? Isn't this the larger goal?

> One is left to wonder what benefits exist for children when the purpose of their artistic endeavours is to create a similar piece as their peers or a replicate of their teacher's creation (closed ended "art") or participate in the same way as the rest of their peers in an activity (scripted, choral performance) …. When children participate in activities that encourage them to copy or produce an adult created or modeled activity, the scope of their creativity is limited, their interpretations of personal and peer work are greatly diminished, and the opportunity for them to enlighten others through a personal discussion of what and how was created is non-existent (Tarr 2001).
>
> (McLennan, 2010)

BUT Kristen, if a child spends all their time making a giant squid, they aren't learning anything else to get them ready for Kindergarten.

The child who made the giant squid learned more that morning that they would have learned in a 1st grade measurement math unit. They learned how to use a tape measure, inches, feet, counting over and over with one-to-one correspondence all the way up to 32, planning, executing a plan, fine motor skills, gross motor skills, crossing the midline, problem solving, visual perception, executive function, self-regulation, and I could go on and on. That is the cool thing about play! It is like opening a world full of learning opportunities that you get to peel through to show others the learning that is happening. It is addicting, and once you see learning (the good sticky kind) through play, you can't unsee it. You will be a believer for life. And then you'll go on to join the play advocate army that is slowly taking over the early childhood world.

BUT Kristen, there are skills that I am teaching through teacher-directed craft projects. It is good practice in following directions. Cutting skills and fine motor skills are things the children get practice in.

Let's be real. Craft projects CAN be good for those things but, in exchange, you are robbing the children of creativity. You may be destroying their own self-confidence because they can't make their paper plate penguin look like yours. They may become frustrated if they can't create something the way the sample looks. Craft projects generally come with a set of rules and guidelines that children must follow in order for their paper plate penguin to turn out "right." If we want children to keep their creativity so they can change the world with new and innovative ideas, we have to let them play and create.

Some teachers may argue that structured crafts are teaching opportunities, or that art centers are too messy for young children, while other teachers buckle under the perceived pressure to promote crafts to satisfy parent requests. However, these types of activities do not allow children to develop problem-solving skills, explore the materials in meaningful ways, or initiate conversations around creating art.

(Galuski & Bardsley, 2015)

If you want them to learn to follow directions, do a morning check-in that includes multiple steps! "Roll the dice, count the spots, and then hop that many times on one foot." Or, when it is time to go to the bathroom and get ready to go outdoors, give them simple directions to follow. And, truth be told, adults are giving children directions ALL DAY LONG everywhere they go so I think that this argument shouldn't even be a thing. They seriously have to practice it all day long. "Get your clothes on and then go brush your teeth." "Get your shoes on, grab your backpack, and then get in the car." "Eat your vegetables before you have your dessert." Point made?

If you want them to learn cutting skills, create a "yes space" in the classroom where they can use scissors on different types of materials! One year, the children at Butterfly Hill were really into cutting everything in the classroom (including my hair) so we created a "yes space" for cutting. I grabbed a plastic kiddie pool, filled it with new things each week and put scissors in there. The children could sit in the pool and cut to their heart's content! (Read more about this in Chapter 5.)

BUT Kristen, we have limited resources so I can't let them squeeze out all the glue.

Yes, sometimes resources are very limited. If this is the case and you can articulate *why* you are saying NO to glue play and it has nothing to do with YOUR need to control the glue and is truly about limited resources, here are some things you can try so you can support the needs and learning of the child.

If squeezing seems to be the child's main goal:

◆ Offer them an old glue bottle that is filled with water in the sensory table or dishpan on the table to squeeze.
◆ If you see many children interested in squeezing the glue, add many different types of squeeze bottles and water to

the sensory table. Ketchup, mustard, and old glue bottles work well for this!
◆ Fill the sensory table with water and give the children sponges in varied sizes and textures for squeezing.

If figuring out how much glue to use is the child's main goal:

◆ Purchase some smaller, reusable bottles and fill them with a bit of watered down glue to make the glue go farther.
◆ Put glue in small silicone cupcake liners or small dixie cups and give the child a paintbrush to use to apply the glue to their project.
◆ Decide how much glue children can use per week to make the glue last. Have a conversation with the children about the resources available for the week and let them know when it is gone, it's gone for the week!

BUT Kristen, if we let one child squeeze out all of the glue, then every child will want to squeeze out all the glue.
Children who have never had uninhibited access to a bottle of glue before will be more inclined to explore by squeezing all of the glue out of the bottle. Not every child will be interested in squeezing out all of the glue, nor will every child have the time and attention it takes to squeeze out a whole bottle of glue. In my experience with freeing the glue, there are only a handful of children that take the time and have the urge to empty a whole bottle of glue. AND, they normally don't do it more than once or twice. The novelty wears off once children realize they have the control of how much glue they can use.

BUT Kristen, the other teachers in the room/school are still in the dot-dot-not-a-lot mindset. How do I explain this concept to them?
As much as we want to, we can't change someone's mind until they are ready to change their own mind. That doesn't mean that we can't model or should give up. Many adults don't even know why they say NO to too much glue.

Here are some things to try:

♦ Discuss with the other adults in the room the possibility of setting up a glue play table for a few weeks as its own "center." Volunteer to monitor and take care of the cleanup.

♦ When making a change, as the late Bev Bos said, "Start in the corner." Start small and expand from there based on the adults' comfort levels. Start with glue in a small container with paint brushes and work up to access to the full bottles.

♦ Take photos of the glue play and create a documentation panel or bulletin board in the classroom that connects the learning happening to early learning standards or benchmarks. This makes the learning visible for the adults who may not see the learning taking place.

References

Galuski, T., & Bardsley, M. (2015). Open-Ended Art: Challenges and Solutions. *Exchange (19460406)*, *226*, 96–99.

Hunter-Doniger, T. (2021). Early Childhood STEAM Education: The Joy of Creativity, Autonomy, and Play. *Art Education*, *74*(4), 22–27. https://doi.org/10.1080/00043125.2021.1905419

Land, G. (2008, November 15). The Failure of Success [Video]. TED Conferences. https://www.ted.com/talks/george_land_the_failure_of_success

McLennan, D. (2010). Process or Product? The Argument for Aesthetic Exploration in the Early Years. *Early Childhood Education Journal*, *38*(2), 81–85. https://doi.org/10.1007/s10643-010-0411-3

Minnesota Department of Education. (2006). *Early Childhood Indicators of Progress: Minnesota's Early Learning Standards*. Minnesota Department of Education.

Perry, B. D. (2001). Curiosity: The Fuel of Development. *Curiosity: The Fuel of Development—Bruce D. Perry, M.D., Ph.D. The Child Trauma Academy Tarrant Cares, Texas*, 2009, tarrant.tx.networkofcare.org/family/library/article.aspx?id=452.

Tok, E. (2022). Early Childhood Teachers' Roles in Fostering Creativity through Free Play. *International Journal of Early Years Education*, *30*(4), 956–968. https://doi.org/10.1080/09669760.2021.1933919

World Economic Forum. (2023). "Future of Jobs: These Are the Most In-Demand Skills in 2023—and Beyond." *World Economic Forum*, www.weforum.org/agenda/2023/05/future-of-jobs-2023-skills/

4

The Hummingbird Teacher

The teacher's role in a child-led, play-based learning environment.

When I was little, I played teacher with a pointer stick, a clipboard, old glasses with the lenses taken out, and a teacher desk situated at the front of my classroom/playroom. I had the students' names all listed out in my grade book that my mom found at a garage sale. My teacher character was the stereotypical teacher one sees on TV or experienced in childhood. My teacher character was loud, strict, and counted to three with her middle finger first (my first grade teacher, Ms. Googe, counted starting with her middle finger first, eliciting giggles from us all). When I was reading the book in front of my class I would lick my finger to turn the page.

When I was teaching in the traditional preschool, I thought that in order for the children to be learning, I had to teach them things. I had to talk, talk, talk all day long and have their attention on me in order for them to be learning. ABCs and 123s were on the lesson plan every day. I thought my voice needed to be louder than the children's voices. I thought that my ideas were better than the children's ideas.

When I was teaching in the traditional preschool classroom, I thought that children needed to practice sitting for long periods of time, so I planned long circle times filled with didactic

DOI: 10.4324/9781003476719-5

(teacher-led) instruction. We did show-and-tell (not developmentally appropriate for four-year-olds and hard to sit through) and storytime, and sometimes I even let them talk (but they had to have the talking stick in order to open their mouth). I was under the impression that I had to spew out all the information and they had to recite things back (including counting at calendar time and the Days of the Week and Months of the Year songs and chants) and be looking at me for learning to happen. I was hugely misinformed on how children construct learning and relied heavily on my own experiences from primary school, and of course teaching my own stuffed animals in my playroom (because that is a super reliable source).

Fast forward to my days teaching at Butterfly Hill in a play-based, child-led program. I was able to shed my teacher character and be fully present in the classroom. That teacher's costume was hung up in the closet never to be seen again. My teaching practice became about becoming a hummingbird teacher and not a helicopter teacher. Let me explain.

A helicopter teacher (like a helicopter parent) is a LOUD presence in the environment. You can't miss it. It is the focal point, and whatever the teacher says, goes. It's all about the teacher in the room and not the children. This lends itself to developmentally inappropriate practice. A hummingbird teacher floats in quietly when needed and floats out just as quickly, being sure not to interrupt or change a child's play. The hummingbird teacher notices when voices become elevated and flutters in closer to see if they are needed. If so, they gently help with problem-solving and then flutter out. The hummingbird teacher provides information when a child wonders about something and asks questions. A hummingbird teacher observes to find out what the children are curious about and then finds opportunities to extend this inquiry. A hummingbird teacher is sneaky and plans out the environment in ways that make children want to find out more or solve problems they happen upon.

One day, when I was hummingbirding about in the indoor classroom, I observed some children throwing bean bags at each other. This was something that could potentially hurt someone so I set up a basket by our back door in a little hallway and told the children they could throw bean bags by the backdoor and challenged them to get the bean bags in the basket from a few feet away. They went about their business and a few minutes later called me over. One of the bean bags got tossed so high that it was now on top of the door opening/closing mechanism. They had thrown a second bean bag up there to try to knock the other one down, but it got stuck too. They asked if I could get the bean bags down, but being a program that is child-centered and encourages learning through trial and error, I asked if they could think of some ways to get them down by saying, "I wonder if you can think of some ways to reach them?" They looked around a bit and one of them suggested they could try standing on a chair to reach them. They moved a little child-sized chair over and one of them got up on the chair. No luck—they weren't tall enough. Another child suggested they get a table to put the chair on to get the bean bags. They worked together to haul a small table over, stacked the chair on top, and crawled up. Still not tall enough. "Do we have a ladder?" asked one of the children. "My great-grandpa has a grabber that he uses to get things off the floor so he doesn't have to bend over. I bet that would work." "Maybe a teacher that has longer arms could get on the table and get it." These are problem-solving skills at work here! Eventually, they settled on finding a child that was taller than them to get up on the chair-table contraption to reach the bean bags.

I could have stepped in and offered assistance. I could have stopped the chair-on-a-table situation because of safety concerns. But, I know that the best learning happens through failure. I also knew they weren't in danger because "hummingbird me" was right in there with them, quietly observing and encouraging. I wanted them to find failure in order for the learning to be more "sticky." In my helicopter teacher days, I would have told the children how to get them down or even just grabbed the bean bags for them. And, just like a helicopter, this blows over the potential for learning. Phrases like "I wonder..." or "What do you think?" are hummingbird teacher questions. In their quiet presence, a hummingbird teacher gives children more to wonder about, more to inquire about, and more to be curious about!

What if I told you that people are completely capable of constructing their own learning? What if I told you that children in groups with varied knowledge and abilities can co-construct learning together? What if I told you that adults aren't necessary all the time for learning to happen? All of these are true.

I came across an experiment done over the course of 20+ years by Sugata Mitra. The experiment is known as The Hole in the Wall Experiment. This experiment started in the late 1990s and revolutionized adults' understanding of children's learning capabilities. Mitra placed computers in public spaces where there were children who didn't go to school and had never seen a computer before. Mitra found that children, left to learn and explore on their own, could learn amazingly well without direct adult instruction. He also found that children have innate curiosity and the ability to self-organize in learning environments. Through collaboration and exploration with other children, they picked up on basic computer literacy skills, navigated educational software, and even did research on various topics using the Internet. This experiment showed us that if children are given access to resources and opportunities, they are fully capable of learning autonomously. Of course, this challenges traditional education that relies heavily on adult-led instruction (Mitra, 2021).

A study by Stipek et al. in 1995 had 227 children participate from 32 preschool and Kindergarten classrooms. The research showed evidence that didactic programs (teacher-directed instruction) provided children with gains over child-centered programs in reading but not in math. The authors found that those gains were outnumbered by many drawbacks of didactic instruction including lower confidence, lower motivation, and higher dependence on adults.

> In educational contexts that allowed children considerable freedom to initiate tasks and complete them without pressure to conform to a particular model or to get right answers, children selected more challenging tasks, were less dependent on an adult for approval, and evidenced more pride in their accomplishment. [...] Didactic instruction is presumed by many experts to inhibit intellectual development directly—by fostering superficial learning

of simple responses rather than real understanding and problem-solving ability—and indirectly, by negatively affecting social-motivational variables which, in turn, affect learning-related behavior (e.g., effort, persistence). For example, experts have argued that didactic, teacher-controlled instruction that emphasizes performance undermines young children's intrinsic interest in learning (Katz, 1988), their perceptions of competence (Kamii, 1985; Katz, 1988), and their willingness to take academic risks (Elkind, 1987).

(Stipek et al., 1995)

When kids have the freedom to choose what they learn, and how they learn it, they tend to tackle more challenging tasks and feel prouder of their accomplishments. On the flip side, rigid instruction that focuses on performance can stifle kids' natural curiosity and willingness to take on new challenges. Teachers need to set the stage and then get out of the way.

BUT Kristen, Vygotsky has clearly found that scaffolding is necessary for children to learn. How does this work if the teacher doesn't directly teach things?

This is where things CAN get a bit tricky. Yes, we know that children learn through scaffolding, which is when a more knowledgeable person (like a teacher) provides guidance and assistance to a learner until they can master a task independently. If a child asks you to teach them how to tie a shoe, you will help them tie a shoe. If a child asks you to help them zip a coat, you teach them how to get the "car in the garage." However, if a child repeatedly asks me to do everything for them, I may see if they can do it on their own. This is where it is SO important to have relationships with each of the children. By knowing their nuances, developmental stage, their likes and dislikes, you will be better able to scaffold their learning when the time is right! We CAN teach things, but in a child-led program the teaching is organic and based on the needs and interests of the children while in play. The teaching will change every day based on the direction the play takes.

BUT Kristen, what if the principal at my school walks by the room and sees children playing. Won't they think that I'm not doing my job?

The honest truth? Yes. They may. And the unfortunate thing that I have seen now that I travel around the United States to speak at schools is that many K-5 principals are getting preschool classrooms added to their job description. It's very likely they haven't completed any courses in early childhood development. If we are being really honest, even if people DO have classes in early childhood, many times play isn't taught. We are up against a machine here. The best advice I can give is to call a meeting with the principal and find out what their viewpoints are. Find out what they know about play. Be an advocate for the children in your class and stand up for them. If *you* don't share how play is essential for development and learning, then who will?

BUT Kristen, what if they aren't ready for Kindergarten when they leave because I didn't teach them anything?

Kindergarten should be ready for them. The adults, policy makers, and administration should be ready for them. But, that doesn't solve the question at hand. You did teach your students! Is it possible there are a few boxes left unchecked as they leave your program and head off to Kindergarten? For sure! But the research tells us that they will learn those remaining pieces when they're developmentally ready to learn them. What you certainly *did* teach your students is confidence, autonomy, motivation to ask questions, willingness to approach a challenge, and persistence in problem-solving. I personally know some adults who have yet to learn these skills. They probably checked all the Kindergarten Readiness boxes!

At some point, I promise, when you have spent time observing children in play and connecting their learning to the early learning standards or benchmarks, you will become a true believer in play. And you will be able to lean fully in and trust all of the research (check out the References of this book) and all of the work psychologists have done so that you can trust yourself and the children. I promise. It takes time, but it will come.

BUT Kristen, is it OK to introduce things to see if children have any interest?

Absolutely! I did this all the time! The really cool thing about wonder is that it is contagious. If I find wonder in the squirrels outside my window, and find awe and curiosity in watching them, it becomes contagious to others around me. When children are curious about something, it will be contagious to you as well! I found wonder in watching monarch caterpillars munch on milkweed all day so I brought them into the classroom to see if the children would be curious as well! They were! That turned into learning about butterflies flying to Mexico. We witnessed the formation of a chrysalis and the subsequent emergence of a butterfly. I introduced a lot of new language and the children LOVED it! When people find wonder, they become curious. When someone is curious, they ask questions and make discoveries. Discovery leads to learning! It is a beautiful cycle, just like the life of a monarch butterfly.

References

Mitra, S. (2021). *The Hole in the Wall: Beginnings of a New Education*. Independently published.

Stipek, D., Feiler, R., Daniels, D., & Milburn, S. (1995). Effects of Different Instructional Approaches on Young Children's Achievement and Motivation. *Child Development*, *66*(1), 209–223. https://doi.org/10.2307/1131201

5

Let Them Pick Their Nose

Children learn so much more when adults learn to say "YES!"

Here is a scene that many of you are familiar with… I sat in front of a group of 20 preschool-aged children, read-singing "There Was an Old Lady Who Swallowed a Fly," when Lo in the back started digging for gold up her little nostrils. Her little finger was the perfect size to fit, her eyes locked on mine as she *really* got in there. I immediately felt my gag reflex knocking on my throat. Without hesitation, I stopped reading and said in front of the whole class, "Lo, finger out of your nose. Now you have germs. Please go wash your hands." I continued on with my book like nothing happened while Lo's face turned red and she shamefully walked to the sink in the back of the classroom. I went on with my day and never thought twice about it. But, Lo. She wasn't able to move on with her day. She had a hard time coming to me for anything after that, choosing instead to approach a different teacher when she needed something or just wanted comfort from an adult. I broke her little spirit that day. It wasn't until my own child experienced something similar that I was able to reflect on the way that I went about telling Lo to stop picking her nose. It struck me deeply when my own child experienced anxiety due to how a teacher addressed them in front of the entire class. I did some rewinding to think about

DOI: 10.4324/9781003476719-6

ways that I had made young children feel ashamed for being human in my presence.

One day I was driving to work and I had some bats in the cave. I took the time to carefully extract the bats (crusty boogers in my nose, if you aren't following me here) with the amazing tool that was put on my hand for just this reason. My finger. Don't even come at me with disgust because I know the majority of you have done it. The little thumb flick on the side of your nostril counts. It was at this moment that I had a revelation. I tell children that picking their nose is gross and germy and shame them. But here I am doing it without even thinking twice about it. And I probably didn't even wash my hands when I got to school. How gross am I? But no one shamed me for it. Being the ever growing and learning teacher that I was, I decided that if I can pick my nose in my car or in the bathroom, I should actually teach children the *appropriate place* to pick their nose in the classroom.

To support their gold-digging adventures I gave children what I call a YES space. I put a small mirror on the wall at child level next to our classroom sink. I named it The Booger Mirror (only in my head because I didn't want children wiping boogers on the mirror) and placed a small table under it topped with a box of tissues. From then on, if I saw a child using their finger to get the boogies, I would quietly direct them to The Booger Mirror and let them know they could pick their nose there. I showed them how to put their booger in a tissue after extraction and directed them to put the tissue in the trash. The last step was for them to wash their hands! Voila. No more shaming for a completely natural bodily function. Let's all admit it here… a three-year-old has a much better outcome when using their finger for the hard ones than when they try blowing into a tissue.

We can apply this concept of a YES space to many other things in the classroom. When we find ways to say YES we are supporting child development, learning, curiosity, child-led learning AND we are reserving our NOs for when it really matters.

Here are some reasons we need to find ways to say YES in our early childhood environments…

By Saying YES, We Are Reserving Our NOs for When a Child Could Be Hurt or Injured

Remember the classic story of the little boy who cried wolf? A shepherd boy cried wolf when there were no wolves around. People got tired of him calling wolf, so when a ferocious wolf actually did show up, no one believed him.

The same is true for young children and the word "NO." An often talked about Harvard survey found the average toddler hears the word NO 400 times per day. When a toddler hears that word SO MANY times a day, the word loses its power. When a caregiver *does* need to use the word when it comes to safety, the children may not listen! We have to reserve our NOs for the moments when there is danger involved and we can learn to say YES in other ways! There are many benefits to saying YES that early childhood educators can take advantage of. Let's break some of them down...

By Saying YES, We Are Meeting the Needs of the Child

Children often communicate their needs through behaviors. By paying attention and responding to these behaviors in a positive, YES way, caregivers can support their learning and development. Let's break this down with an example. Picture a toddler climbing a shelf in the classroom. Generally, if we have said NO to this behavior over and over, we may think the child is trying to misbehave on purpose when in fact the child could be:

- ◆ **Expressing Curiosity:** Children have a natural desire to explore the environment around them, including vertically (whether we are comfortable with it or not)!
- ◆ **Seeking a Challenge:** The child could be showing a need for challenges and opportunities to test their physical abilities and take risks!
- ◆ **Building Confidence:** If a child is repeatedly trying to climb all the things, the child could need support and encouragement in mastering a new skill. This helps develop their self-confidence! The "I did it" moment!!

- ◆ **Sensory Input and Exploration:** The child could be communicating a need for sensory exploration. Climbing gives young children opportunities for tactile experiences and the development of sensory processing skills.
- ◆ **Body Autonomy:** The child could be showing a need for autonomy and independence! They are learning to take control and make decisions about their own actions.

By Saying YES, We Are Encouraging Curiosity and Creativity

Remember the story about the Glue Plate back in Chapter 3? If I had said "dot-dot-not-a-lot" and said NO to squeezing out all the glue, Lo (and our whole class) would never have had the amazing learning experience we shared! By saying YES, her creative juices were allowed to flow freely. And the bonus cherry on top was seeing the inquisitiveness and questioning that happened along the Glue Plate journey! AND, now that we know that children lose their creativity as they enter elementary school, it is essential that we give them full autonomy over their creative endeavors!

By Saying YES, We Are Supporting Child-led Learning!

If we pay attention, children will show us what they are interested and curious about through their actions in the classroom. A true child-led program is a developmentally appropriate program. Children will always show us what they need, what they are interested in, and what their mind and body are ready to learn and explore. We just have to pay attention and be detectives!

By Saying YES, We Can Redirect Undesirable Behaviors that Aren't Conducive to the Time and Space Available

Sometimes we may not have time to say YES to something. Or, maybe the space we have available isn't set up in a way that can support some things children are drawn to exploring. If we can find a way to say YES in a different way, we are supporting a child's needs and curiosity AND encouraging child-led learning. We're saying, "I see your need, and I'm going to help you find a safe way to explore it."

Now that I have explained the reasons we should find ways to say YES in our classrooms, I would like to give you some examples of *how* to say YES!

Change the Environment

My Play Fareygawdmather (that spelling is right!), Lisa Murphy says, "Change the environment, not the child." If running in the classroom is something that a teacher normally says NO to, one strategy is to find a way to change the environment (which may, in turn, shut down the unwanted behavior).

When a child is at the end of a hallway in a hotel, we all know they take off and start running down the hallway. The hallway is inviting them to RUN! This could be true in the classroom as well. If the tables are set up in a way that looks like a racetrack, that racetrack is screaming at children, "Run around me!!" To change the environment, a teacher could strategically place shelves, or arrange the tables so the racetrack disappears making it harder and less inviting to run.

This can be done in many different areas and ways. If a caregiver is tired of telling toddlers not to climb on a shelf, turn the shelf around. By being strategic about the way the environment is set up, a teacher can negate some of the behaviors they get tired of saying NO to continually.

Change the Location (Think Booger Mirror Here)

One year, we had a class of children that were very interested in cutting everything they weren't supposed to cut. Hair, the classroom rug, clothes. Instead of taking all the scissors away, I decided to give the children a place where they COULD cut. I brought in a blue plastic kiddie pool and named it The Cutting Pool. Each week we would fill it with something different that the children could cut, and put scissors in the pool. The children could sit in the pool and cut the materials in the pool. We filled it with birthday party streamer rolls, straws, old book orders and magazines, fabric scraps, leaves, old bulletin board borders, wallpaper samples, paint samples, and so many more things! We also still had scissors on the process art shelves, but by giving the children an interesting place to cut interesting things, we eliminated the rug cutting and hair cutting!

By changing the location we were able to stop the cutting of all the things they shouldn't be cutting in our classroom and encourage them in a creative way to continue practicing their scissor skills, fine motor, and hand–eye coordination in a different place in the classroom.

Give a Choice or an Alternative

Children engaging in the filling and dumping play schema might empty all the baskets of loose parts onto the floor while they explore. If we want to stop them from dumping all the loose parts out, we can give them some other choices. Tell the child, "I see you are having fun dumping out the baskets! Someone could slip and fall on all of these things. You can either dump water in the sink or you use a small dump truck in the sensory table with beans! Which would you like to do?"

By giving them a choice we are supporting their learning, still giving them some autonomy with the choices and also negating the unwanted behavior (the dumping of the loose parts baskets).

Children LOVE to color and paint on their own skin with markers and paint. If this is a limit in the classroom, a way to say YES is to get a hairstyling mannequin head (the kind with real hair that cosmetologists use to practice on) and allow the children to paint the mannequin's face and hair. Then, throw the head in the sensory table with some water and baby shampoo and allow the children to scrub it clean. You could also print out a large photo of the child's face and let them paint the photo of their own face. By giving an alternative, we are supporting their needs and interests and allowing them the chance to explore and learn.

BUT Kristen, if I say YES all the time I am just letting children do whatever they want, when they want, and that isn't going to fly in my classroom.

A YES environment doesn't mean an environment without limits and boundaries. A teacher can still hold limits and boundaries in the classroom. With any rule or limit put in place, I encourage you to reflect on why the limits and boundaries are in place. A lot of the behaviors in the classroom that we often say "no" to or find frustrating are completely normal and developmentally appropriate for the age group of children we are working with. It is our job to support them AND keep them safe. You can have a limit that children can't throw anything indoors if safety is involved, but then children should have the opportunity to throw things outdoors. You can tell children NO to climbing up the slide because children are going down, but provide one day a week when they *can* go up the slide.

BUT Kristen, if we say YES to everything there isn't any structure and children need structure.

When this question pops up in relation to saying YES, I like to flip the question around. A lot of times the word "structure" is thrown around and we don't really peel it apart to know what it truly means. Many times adults say "structure" when they really mean control. Adults love to control their environment, and they looooove to control children. I encourage you to think about this in a different way. Are you wanting CONTROL over the classroom and children when you say "they need structure," or are you implying they need a routine and predictability in their day? In a YES environment we can still have predictability and routines! But we need to let go of our need for control and allow children to lead their own learning.

BUT Kristen, if we say YES to everything, how will they learn how to act properly in a classroom when they leave our program and start Kindergarten?

Here's the deal, Kindergarten is not ready for them. We need to allow children to have three-year-old experiences, four-year-old experiences, and five-year-old experiences. If we spend our time providing watered down Kindergarten curriculum, we are taking away their chance to learn in a developmentally appropriate way. We are doing a disservice to the children in our care when we are planning for the next stage and not letting them live in the stage they are currently in. Just because children will eventually need to master a skill doesn't mean it's appropriate for preschool. It's why we don't have our three-year-olds practice filing their income taxes!

Most children aren't ready for the long sitting times, lack of play, worksheets, and teacher-directed activities that are a staple of traditional Kindergarten classrooms. Most children will have a hard time with Kindergarten expectations no matter if they are in a YES environment or a traditional preschool environment. I want to know that I have done everything I could to provide the most developmentally appropriate learning environment for children while they were in my care.

BUT Kristen, if you let children pick their nose, how will they ever learn to blow their nose?

I hardly ever use a tissue to blow my nose unless I have a cold and the snot is runny. And apparently, according to a very accurate poll on social media (a hint of sarcasm here), most other adults pick their nose as well (so I am not gross). It is *way* easier to use a finger to get the really stuck, hard ones out. Blowing the nose is a hard concept to understand when you are three years old. Haven't you ever held a tissue up to a child's nose and said "blow" and the tissue sucked up their nostrils as they took a big breath in? They WILL learn to blow their nose eventually and you CAN introduce the strategies to shooting air out their nostrils, but it takes practice, and for some it comes much later than preschool.

6

The Great Worm Saving Expedition

Children learn best through real-world adventures.

As I rolled up to Butterfly Hill a few years ago, it was raining. It was a nice light rain but it had downpoured at some point during the night. As I got out of my car, ready to set my foot on the pavement, I saw worms. Worms were everywhere. Some were wiggly, some were smashed, some were drowning in puddles of water. I reached down to save the worms struggling in the water and wished that I could save every worm from getting driven over on the parking lot. I have a lot of empathy for worms after storms for some reason. I mean, their whole home was probably destroyed and they don't have a worm emergency hotline.

I went in to get the room set up for the day and decided on a morning check-in that got the children thinking about what they noticed on their short walk into school from the parking lot. Would they notice the worms too? Morning check-in is something we did each morning as children were welcomed into the school. It's a short one-on-one interaction for each child and the greeting teacher. This morning in particular I wanted to see if the children could draw a worm on the white board. I wanted to check in to see if a child could hold a writing utensil with a decent grasp,

DOI: 10.4324/9781003476719-7

use shapes or lines to represent an idea or object, and I wanted to see if they could start waving their line up and down, as this shows more control of the utensil and body. I asked, "Did you notice anything in the parking lot on your way into the school?" Most children had noticed the worms, so I invited them to draw what they saw (of course some worms were flat with guts on the whiteboard—but, hey—that means they are able to communicate their ideas through their pictures!). Some children drew a little dash, some drew a wavy line, and some drew 3D-looking worms with faces. One child drew a worm and said, "My worm looks like the letter W!" I was elated they made this observation, and to scaffold a bit I said, "Do you know what letter the word WORM starts with?" The child didn't know, so I said, "It starts with W! Worm starts with W and you just said your picture of a worm looks like a W!" The child's eyes lit up with awe and they started to make more W worms on the white board.

Once all the children were at school and we had a dazzling display of dead and alive worms on the whiteboard, I asked if any kiddos wanted to head outside in the rain to go on a Worm Saving Expedition. About 15 kiddos decided to get suited up in their rain gear to head outdoors with me and another teacher. The children started collecting all of the living worms they could. Their hands were getting full, so one child asked for a bucket to put them in. We grabbed a bucket from the outdoor classroom. The bottom of the bucket was a wriggly, wet, wormy mess and children were using language like, "It's getting full!" and "They are so slimy!" and they started to make observations like, "Some of these worms are a lot bigger than the other ones." Questions were asked like, "Why do the big ones get all slimy when you pick them up?" What happened next still has me in awe of what children are capable of when given time to explore.

A child asked for another bucket so they could separate the big worms (the invasive nightcrawlers that fisherpeople love) and the little earthworms (the worms the gardeners love). While some children kept up the Worm Saving Expedition, a few sat down on the ground to work to separate the big worms from the small worms. They dumped out the bucket into the grass and started counting as they put them back in the buckets, one by one. One child kept track of how many big worms they had and one kept track of how many little worms they put back in the bucket. It became a worm competition, and the children started gathering around to count together as one child separated out the pile, one by one. They counted (with a teeny bit of help to keep the numbers straight) to over 100 for the small worms and about 40 for the big worms. Then a child noticed that the buckets looked like they had the same amount of worms. Another child piped in to say, "The bigger worms take up more space so it looks like there are the same number." Woah.

Real, sticky learning happens by doing.

> Play is not frivolous; it is brain building. Play has both direct and indirect effects on brain structure and functioning. Play leads to changes at the molecular (epigenetic), cellular (neuronal connectivity), and behavioral levels (social-emotional and executive functioning skills) that promote learning and adaptive and/or prosocial behavior (Yogman et al., 2018).
>
> (Swart & Houser, 2023)

We ended up dumping the bucket of smaller worms out into the outdoor classroom and we packed up the nightcrawlers with some newspaper and put them in the fridge to be used for fishing (don't worry, they are super invasive and we have to keep them out of the ground so fishing is the best end-of-life decision for them).

Compare this totally organic, child-led morning with placing a worksheet in front of a child. Maybe it's a worksheet with the letter W the children get to trace over and over. The child sits at a table, uses a small pencil to trace the letter W a few times and then colors in a picture of a worm. Sounds so exciting, right? Nope. Between these two experiences, which one do you think promotes lifelong learning? "Theory and research strongly support the benefits of play and since play provides children with opportunities to explore and interact with the world around them, it is not surprising there is a link between play experiences during early childhood and later school success" (Fisher et al., 2011)" (Swart & Houser, 2023).

For the sake of making a point, let's compare the learning/ practicing that is happening during each of these activities in Table 6.1. The benchmarks in this breakdown come from the Minnesota Early Childhood Indicators of Progress (Minnesota Department of Education, 2006).

If this list doesn't convince you to burn all the worksheets in your classroom, I am not sure I will be able to help change your mind. While a child may practice a handful of skills with a worksheet, they are experiencing and practicing so many more with real world, curiosity-inducing, play-based learning experiences (like the Worm Saving Expedition). And guess what! You won't have the classroom management problems that generally come from making children sit and do worksheets! I have seen this firsthand after teaching in a traditional way (complete with mandatory long circle time, calendar time, and craft projects) vs. allowing children the freedom to play and construct their own learning! When children are able to choose developmentally appropriate activities and how they spend their time in play, they are generally MUCH happier (Zhbanova et al., 2010).

Think of it this way: If your boss tells you that you have to follow their plan and their forms and their way of doing things, you may roll your eyes and want to buck the system. Your brain may think differently and you may be more efficient or motivated to do something in a different way. Most humans like autonomy over how they spend their time and how they choose to work. Children are no different. They thrive when they have autonomy over their time and experiences. When other people step in to tell them how to do something, or that they HAVE to do something, motivation fades, curiosity diminishes, and the learning is not as deep and well rounded!

Worksheets may provide a way to show families what their child did at preschool. Worksheets are used as receipts that say, "Hey, I'm a real teacher and I'm getting them ready for Kindergarten! I taught your child the letter W today!" Worksheets are a stereotypical classroom staple in schools everywhere. Parents may even proudly display a W worksheet on the fridge. But is there another way to teach the same thing? "Studies that compared the performance of children attending academic preschools with

Letter W Worksheet	Worm Saving Expedition
• Shows interest in and associates sounds with words	• Shows interest in and associates sounds with words
• Recognizes how features of a letter combine to make a specific letter	• Recognizes how features of a letter combine to make a specific letter
• Uses letter-like symbols to make letters or words	• Uses letter-like symbols to make letters or words
• Draws letters and/or part of name with some reversals	• Draws letters and/or part of name with some reversals
• Grasps a crayon to scribble/color	• Use observation to develop an accurate description of natural phenomena and compare one's observational and descriptive with those of others
	• Grasps a crayon to scribble/color
	• Sorts objects based on an observable attributes
	• Sort objects using characteristics such as shape, size, color, and thickness
	• Participates in simple data collection discussed by an adult or other child
	• Identifies patterns, differences, or similarities of information collected
	• Assists with putting boots on and taking off
	• Puts on coat and takes coat off with assistance
	• Verbally identifies obvious differences and similarities
	• Expresses curiosity and/or formulates questions of complex concepts
	• Seeks to gain additional knowledge in areas of interest
	• Monitor daily and seasonal changes in weather and summarize changes
	• Sort objects in terms of color, size, shape, and texture and communicate reasoning for the sorting system
	• Use words to compare objects according to length, size, weight and position
	• Shows understanding of measurement terms (longer/shorter, taller/shorter, fullest, farthest, closest)
	• Compares and orders more than two items in some way
	• Talks with others about questions, actions, ideas, observations, or results

- Verbally expresses ideas/thought process
- Scribbles or draws to show and/or share ideas
- Uses prior experience to identify details that may be relevant
- Makes self-directed choices from a greater variety of options
- Sustains attention and persistence with a task of interest for at least 5 minutes
- Shares information and participates in activities with adults and peers
- Shows concern, respect, care, and appreciation for others and the environment
- Identifies and describes significant objects and places in familiar environments
- Uses simple physical strategies to combine or separate sets
- States the number that comes next or before up to 10
- Uses terms like more/less; bigger/smaller; a little bit/a lot; to refer to approximate quantities
- Demonstrates and uses 1:1 correspondence with sets larger than four
- Recites number word aloud, forward, up to at least 29 (allow for some mistakes), without objects
- Recites number words but not necessarily in the correct order
- Uses letter-like symbols to make letters or words
- Uses scribbles, shapes, or pictures to represent thoughts and ideas
- Uses drawing to represent writing
- Points to and names some letters (especially in their own name)
- Uses sentences that express logical relationships between concepts

TABLE 6.1 Breakdown of learning benchmarks achieved during each activity

Source: Minnesota Department of Education, 2006.

those attending play-based preschools showed no advantage in reading and math achievement for children attending academic preschools" (Swart & Houser, 2023). OK, what?? If we're not doing W worksheets to increase student achievement, then why are we doing them at all? We can learn about the letter W while having fun with worms!

Children in a developmentally appropriate setting hone their creativity and confidence. They learn to bravely walk into an environment, assess their own needs, and seek out resources. Show me a preschool worksheet that teaches those skills!

How can we keep filling out children's time with teacher-directed learning experiences like worksheets and flashcards when there are mounds of evidence that argue for play-based experiences in early childhood? This trickle down of using worksheets in early childhood is stealing valuable learning time from our children! "[A] preponderance of research has shown that there is a false dichotomy between rigorous academic learning and play.… Students are more likely to learn important academic skills and content through play than by having teacher-directed instruction outside of a playful context, as with, for instance, the filling out of a worksheet" (Lieberman & Cook, 2016, p. 9). Woah.

When early childhood educators (and parents, too!) can step back from what their own experiences in early childhood and school were like and trust the work of scholars, researchers, and psychologists, we can throw out the rote learning experiences like worksheets and replace them with play-based learning experiences. Worksheets don't offer children social and emo-tional experiences. They don't offer much in the way of critical or divergent thinking. They don't offer a connection to the child's interests. They don't offer the development of executive function or self-regulation skills. They don't offer anything other than a quick receipt that the teacher did something academic-y in the eyes of the adults outside the classroom. In fact, when parents understand the power of play, their child's development is better supported! (Swart & Houser, 2023) This is why it is essential to observe and document learning that happens through play (see more on this in Chapter 7). Say goodbye to W worksheets on the fridge, and hello to worm buckets and stick squiggles drawn in the mud!

But Kristen, I teach in a program that has a curriculum we have to follow, and worksheets are included in that.
There is a lot to unpack here. If you know that worksheets aren't developmentally appropriate yet are required in the program you are teaching in, what are you doing about it? Nothing will change if us knowers don't stand up and advocate for the children we are serving. We are doing our children a disservice if we aren't advocating for what we know is developmentally appropriate and supported by research. Here are a couple of advocacy tips:

♦ Head to the References at the end of each chapter and grab the articles and research that have been cited. Schedule a meetup with the admin making the curriculum decisions and present your findings. Ask them to provide research or other evidence that worksheets are a better option than play in early childhood classrooms.

♦ Observe and document learning that is happening through play. You can start with your own version of the Worksheet–Worm table chart from this chapter (Table 6.1)! Connect the learning to your state's or country's early learning standards or benchmarks to make it visible for the adults outside the room. Do the same for a worksheet and the learning that is happening through a child completing a worksheet. Let them see the differences in learning between child-led play experiences and rote learning activities.

In the meantime, get creative. Can you laminate the worksheets and offer them as a choice for children to do during free play? If a child chooses to complete the worksheet all on their own, that is play! Some children may eat it up and, if they are choosing to do it, they may have a friend doing it too. The social play that happens while they complete their play worksheets is gold and should be celebrated as well!

BUT Kristen, I have used worksheets for years and the children really love them!

My question is, have you asked each and every child that? Do you really know they LOVE them or would they rather be in play? If they had 14 other play-based experiences to choose from, would they choose the worksheets? If this is the mindset you have, I am urging you to reflect on your practice and why YOU are holding on to things that are not developmentally appropriate and don't serve the children in the highest capacity. Is it easier? Is it because you have always done it that way? Is it because you grew up doing worksheets and liked them? Is it because you have never considered that children can actually learn through play (and learn better)? What idea has you clutching those worksheets? Unpack that.

My Play Fareygawdmather, Lisa Murphy, often states that there are three questions to answer when designing or planning an experience in the early childhood classroom: What am I doing? Why am I doing it? Who is it for? (Murphy, 2020). Lisa suggests that if your answer is "I don't know" to any of the questions, stop immediately. You aren't allowed to do it if you can't articulate why. "Why? Because if you know what you are doing and why you are doing it and who it's for, you are being genuinely *intentional* in your practice" (Murphy, 2020). And that is where you want to be!

> Otherwise we could simply just be going through the motions, disconnected from the WHAT or a WHY, perhaps just doing something because it has become a habit or routine. Maybe someone told us that's how it had to be done, so we signed on, signed up and just got with the program without ever questioning anything.
>
> (Murphy, 2020)

I'm raising my hand. That was me. I just did what I knew! What I had experienced in my own school journey. What I thought parents/guardians wanted to see. When I leaned into play, I was really able to start questioning everything (with the help of Lisa's Three Questions) and weeding out all of the things that don't serve children in a developmentally appropriate way. I encourage you to start this reflective practice as well!

BUT Kristen, my child sees their older sibling doing worksheets and wants to do their own worksheets. Should I not let them?
 If a child has been exposed to worksheets and asks for them, that is play for that child so I would support their play!

References

Lieberman, A., & Cook, S. (2016). (rep.). *A FALSE DICHOTOMY: Elementary Principals on Academics and Play Acknowledgments About New America About the Education Policy Program*. New America.

Minnesota Department of Education. (2006). *Minnesota Early Childhood Indicators of Progress*. Minnesota Department of Education.

Murphy, L. (2020). *Lisa Murphy on Being Child Centered*. Redleaf Press.

Swart, K., & Houser, K. (2023). Early Childhood Play and Academics: What Are Parents' Perceptions? *Dimensions of Early Childhood*, *51*(2), 28–32.

Zhbanova, K., Rule, A., Montgomery, S., & Nielsen, L. (2010). Defining the Difference: Comparing Integrated and Traditional Single-Subject Lessons. *Early Childhood Education Journal*, *38*(4), 251–258. https://doi.org/10.1007/s10643-010-0405-1

7

Play Detectives

Unveiling the genius in children's play by observing and documenting.

One evening, my colleague and I decided to hide 1,200 rubber ducks in all different colors in the outdoor classroom of Butterfly Hill! They were all the same size but came in about ten different colors. Can you imagine the awe and wonder that crossed the children's faces as they took to the grass that morning seeing the ducks hiding everywhere? I did this with a specific goal in mind. I know that children are natural mathematicians and will count, sort, and compare large quantities of similar objects. Well, my sneakiness paid off!

While the children collected ducks, the teachers could see that some children were collecting only certain colors. Some were finding colors for their friends and some didn't care what color they got, they just wanted as many as they could find! After many were collected, some children counted to determine who had the most (one-to-one correspondence), who had the most of a particular color (comparing/contrasting), and then they set out to use them in their play. Some children carried them around in buckets all day (transporting schema) and some laid them out on giant cookie sheets in the mud kitchen in rows separated by

DOI: 10.4324/9781003476719-8

color (positioning schema, sorting/classifying, planning and organizing). The teachers could see all of the organic learning and practicing that was happening while they observed the children in play!

Back in my traditional preschool teaching days, I created an assessment to complete by pulling out individual children during their free play time. The children had to tell me what letters they knew as I flashed them one by one, count as high as they could, trace letters on a piece of paper, cut on a straight and curvy line, and identify shapes and letter sounds. In my quest to look and sound like a "real" teacher, I took children from play and quizzed them on academic skills. I based this assessment on what I thought a child should know before Kindergarten, yet I hadn't even looked into DAP and the importance of whole child development in the early years. I hadn't even cracked open the Minnesota Early Childhood Indicators of Progress (ECIPs; my state's early learning benchmarks). How could I possibly design our time together if I didn't even have a blueprint to follow? Looking back on it, I placed a HUGE emphasis on cognitive development and hardly any time on the rest of the whole-child-pie domains of early learning! I saw a child's accomplishments and struggles based on only one (very academic-focused) piece of the whole-child-pie. It wasn't until I started observing and documenting children in play that I was able to open my eyes to the amazing amount of learning that takes place during child-led free play, across all domains of early childhood development. The evidence was in front of me the whole time, and I didn't need to pull out children from their play to see it!

Most of us have gone through an industrialized model of the education system. We were "taught to the test." If I had to go back and take my 10th grade chemistry test right now, I would fail miserably even though I aced it at the time. I probably spent hours memorizing the periodic table of elements, but 30 years later I only know H_2O and CO_2. Did I actually learn and understand it, or was I just memorizing something I didn't truly understand OR care about? The latter seems to be true! The argument can be made that it is important to expose students to a variety of topics so they can find information and ways of learning that suit them. Some people go on to study organic chemistry at a university because of a spark that ignited in high school Intro to Chemistry, right? We do exactly that with our differentiated learning areas and play provocations in the preschool classroom (see Chapter 2).

Formal assessments, tests, or even worksheets are not developmentally appropriate for young children. Often, when children are asked to perform and spit out knowledge for a teacher-led assessment, the teacher is only looking for cognitive-based skills and overlooks all of the other things that make each child unique and motivated! And, giving young children tests can lead to lifelong test anxiety!

> Studies that compared the performance of children attending academic preschools with those attending play-based preschools … did suggest that children attending academic preschools had higher levels of test anxiety, were less creative, and had more negative attitudes toward school than did the children attending play-based preschool.
>
> (Swart & Houser, 2023)

The way I pulled children from play to quiz them on skills and knowledge is not the most effective way to get a well-rounded picture of each child's growth and development. Research done in Reggio, Montessori and Waldorf/Steiner programs has shown that assessment is most effective when it is developmentally appropriate, child-centered, and focused on dispositions and engagements.

> Because authentic assessment emphasizes the individual child, the feedback that it encourages teachers to give is often activity, rather than outcome, focused. This form of feedback encourages children's continued engagement with a variety of materials rather than children being able to recite back certain information (DeLuca et al., 2019). In our current test-based culture, undue emphasis is placed on assessing what has been learned, putting limited

emphasis on the process of learning (Frans et al., 2020; Stiggins, 2005).

(Becker et al., 2022)

The second year Butterfly Hill was open, I decided to dive deep into documentation, emphasizing the learning process over outcomes, which is a departure from traditional assessments. The other teachers and I committed to nine months of observation and documentation. By this point in time, our program was rumored to be known as the "hippie preschool," or the preschool where they "just let children play and do whatever they want." I wanted to prove to the adults outside our walls that play is the most developmentally appropriate way to teach young children. We needed to make the learning process visible to them! The teachers and I downloaded an app to document learning that I aligned with the Minnesota Early Childhood Indicators of Progress. We took photos and videos of children in play and then connected the learning happening to the ECIPs. These photos and videos were sent off to the parents/guardians each day so they could see the learning taking place, even if nothing was going home in their child's backpack!

I already believed in play-based learning, but by taking time to observe children in play and connecting that learning to the Minnesota Early Childhood Indicators of Progress, I was able to tangibly share with adults the amazing amounts of learning taking place in all the domains of early childhood education! I became addicted to extracting the learning and making it visible to other adults. It was a creative experience and play for me! After spending nine months in a full-on, deep dive into documentation every day, I was a fierce advocate (with evidence in-hand) in the power of play! If you are on the fence about how children learn through play, I invite you to challenge yourself and commit to observing and documenting children in play. Once you see the play connect to the learning and practicing the children are doing, you can't unsee it! Documentation is the story of a child's learning and is the most developmentally appropriate way to assess a child's learning and progress.

What Is Observation in Relation to Teaching in an Early Childhood Environment?

Observation may seem like it is a simple concept; sit back, drink coffee, and watch the children playing, right? Nope. Observation is so much more complex than that. By being intentional in our observations we can get a bird's eye view of each child's development and learning! Observation in early childhood education is a systematic and purposeful way of looking at, listening to, and noting the behaviors, actions, expressions, and interactions of children as they engage in activities and with their environment through play! But don't let that scare you away—most teachers do these things naturally and make these connections about children just by being aware and present.

Why Is Observation So Important in Early Childhood Environments?

According to Dr. Hilary Seitz, "The process of authentic assessment helps to shift the concept of assessment from a narrow view of comparing children with numbers that reflect what they do not know to a system that demonstrates what children do know and can do (Escamilla 2021)" (Seitz, 2023).

To put it bluntly, formal assessments highlight what a child *can't* do, while observation and documentation show what a child CAN do! Observation is important for all of the following reasons:

- ◆ **Awareness of Each Child's Learning Across All Domains:** Through observation, caregivers can track the developmental progress of each child including physical, cognitive, social, and emotional and creative development. This helps us make sure that there aren't any big pieces of the whole-child-pie missing!
- ◆ **Individualized Learning:** Observation allows teachers to understand the unique learning styles, interests, needs

and strengths of each child. By being in-tune with these things for each child, teachers can design personalized learning experiences that take into account each child's unique needs and interests. Curating individualized learning experiences leads to more evidence!

◆ **Evidence of Learning:** Regular observations provide concrete evidence of a child's growth over time. A teacher can also discover what areas a child may be less confident or less interested in and can then plan ahead to provide differentiated instruction for that child. For example, if a child LOVES matchbox cars and never leaves the rug as they play with cars, a teacher could create a car parking lot on cardboard with numbers in the spaces and correlating numbers on the top of each car. The teacher can observe the child in play to see if they make the number connection!

◆ **Planning the Learning Environment:** Observations help educators evaluate the effectiveness of the learning environment and materials available in the classroom. Insights gained from observing children in play can help us plan an environment that induces creativity and engages children based on their interest, needs, learning styles, and strengths! At Butterfly Hill, the "lesson" plans are not actually based on lessons to teach. The teachers plan for the environment based on what they observed from the children's play (more on that in Chapter 2).

◆ **Supporting Social and Emotional Development:** When we observe children in play, we can gain insights into children's social interactions, emotional expressions, and how they navigate conflicts and challenges. We can plan ahead for dysregulated children based on what we observe.

◆ **Facilitating Parent/Guardian–Teacher Communication:** Observations provide concrete examples of learning through play that teachers can share with parents/guardians, offering a glimpse into their child's day, progress, and experiences in the classroom. The connection teachers have with the grown ups at home supports the child's overall development at home and at school!

Observation in early childhood education is not just about sitting back and watching children while drinking coffee and chatting with your co-teacher, but involves a thoughtful and intentional process of understanding each child deeply. It supports educators in creating a nurturing, inclusive, and stimulating environment that respects and responds to the needs and potential of every child. Practicing observation is *fundamental* for early childhood educators because it informs decision-making and reflective teaching practices that are essential for the best whole-child-pie development and learning in young children.

How Does a Teacher Observe and Document during Play?

Every teacher will find their own ebb and flow and their own creative process for observation and documentation. What worked for me, could work for you… but it also may not. The processes of observation and documentation are unique to each teacher and I encourage you to find a way to observe and document that works for you.

I liked to think of myself as a play detective when I observed children in play. I went on stakeouts for learning! My stakeouts may have lasted a few minutes when I noticed something amazing happening at the sensory table with two children, or the stakeout could last 20 minutes while I monitored the crayon melting station and each child passing through. I took notes on paper that I found lying around somewhere (but you can keep a notebook or clipboard in the classroom to help you stay organized) to help me remember what I observed later in the day when I was connecting the learning happening to the early learning standards. Capturing learning moments with photos and videos was essential so I could show the learning taking place to the adults outside the classroom via the photo sharing app.

In the preschool program I founded, I experimented with various methods of documenting learning throughout my years of teaching. The following are ways that I tried out and you may choose to try as well!

◆ **Documentation Panels:** Documentation panels are visual displays that show children's projects, artwork, photographs, and learning experiences. These panels often include children's quotes, teachers' observations, work samples, and explanations (I call them learning stories) of the learning process. Documentation panels are usually placed on a wall making the learning visible to parents, children (they love to see their own work and photos on the wall), and other educators. Documentation panels can be thematic (writing samples found around the classroom), focusing on a specific project or exploration (glue sculptures) or they can document an ongoing learning process (name writing).

◆ **Floorbooks/Class Journals:** Floorbooks are large, scrapbook-style books that capture children's voices, ideas, questions, and reflections on their learning journey. Created collaboratively by children and caregivers, floorbooks can be used as a tool during group discussions or group/circle time, allowing children to contribute their own thoughts, work samples, and drawings! They are an excellent tool for child-led learning as you can see in real time where children's interests lie! When I used this method, I would leave the journal/floorbook out for the families to see when they would pick up their child at the end of each day. Children also loved to look back at the things we had done in the past.

◆ **Photo/Video Apps:** Photo and video apps are digital tools that allow teachers to capture, organize, and share moments of children's learning quickly and efficiently with the people outside the classroom. This was my go-to documentation style, but I always made sure I waited until I wasn't with the children to add the notes, connect the learning standards, or write the learning stories to go along with photos and videos (children see adults on screens too much as it is). This documentation style allows for a deeper school-to-home connection!

◆ **Social Media:** Using social media platforms as a documentation strategy involves creating private groups or pages where the teachers can share updates, photos, videos, and learning highlights with the children's families and the school community. This form of documentation promotes transparency, allows for real-time updates about what the children are interested in and learning, and can encourage engagement and feedback from families. Please always remember that it is essential to ensure privacy and consent when sharing children's learning experiences on social media.

◆ **Student Journals:** Student journals are personalized books or folders where children can document their learning experiences, thoughts, and reflections through drawings, writing, and storytelling. At Butterfly Hill Nature Preschool, each child is given a 6 × 9 journal with unlined pages and their photo and name on the front. They can use their journal in any way they choose. Most children choose to draw, make marks, write their name over and over, or write any words or letters they know. The teachers encourage the children to tell stories that the teacher will dictate. It is fun to see the stories change and get more detailed as the children grow! The journals are sent home with the children when they leave us to head to the big school world and are a great keepsake for the families.

Though this is not a comprehensive list of documentation methods, maybe this list will help you get creative and find some new inspiration into the world of being a play detective!

◆ **Morning Check-In:** This is a brief one-on-one moment with each child as they enter the classroom before they become engaged in play. This is a planned activity used to check understanding as each of the children comes into school for the day. If you need to find out if the children can count to ten, you could give them a set of ten Duplo® blocks and have them count them as they connect them together. (Remember white board worms in Chapter 6?) Assessments can still be done; we just have to get creative about it so as to not pull children from their play.

And if you make it more fun than having them recite letters from flashcards, the children won't feel as much pressure to perform!

BUT Kristen, the children have so many needs during play and I feel like I am always playing referee so I don't have time to observe... what then?

Part of our job as early childhood educators is to provide care for the children and their needs. By taking time to walk children through social situations (and emotional ones too), as well as help children take care of their basic needs, we ARE observing AND building relationships with those kiddos. And it is through relationships that reflective observation starts.

BUT Kristen, the curriculum we use forces us to pull the children to assess them one by one. What can I do to make this more developmentally appropriate?

Just as you are a play detective, you can be an assessment ninja. Take the form you are to complete for each child and put it on a clipboard. Sneak in and observe when they're at the process art table, jotting down things on a clipboard or when you hear them counting something at the sensory table! Keep a clipboard for yourself handy to jot down notes so you don't forget to go into that child's assessment form and check it off later on!

References

Becker, I., Rigaud, V. M., & Epstein, A. (2022). Getting to Know Young Children: Alternative Assessments in Early Childhood Education. *Early Childhood Education Journal*, *51*(5), 911–923. https://doi.org/10.1007/s10643-022-01353-y

Seitz, H. (2023). Authentic Assessment: A Strengths-Based Approach to Making Thinking, Learning, and Development Visible. *YC: Young Children*, *78*(1), 6–11.

Swart, K., & Houser, K. (2023). Early Childhood Play and Academics: What Are Parents' Perceptions? *Dimensions of Early Childhood*, *51*(2), 28–32.

8

Yesteryear and Tomorrowday

Traditional calendar time is like trying to teach a preschooler quantum physics!

Imagine trying to teach a three-year-old to swim by showing them pictures of swimming pools and asking them to recite swimming techniques while they sit on a carpet square in a classroom. They might repeat back the names of strokes, but they're missing the splash and giggles that make swimming fun. They don't know how to take those strokes and make themselves float. They're missing the connection!

Forty two hours. That is an estimate of the number of hours a child will sit through calendar time in two years of preschool at ten minutes a day, four days a week, 32 weeks out of the year. If you ask any five-year-old what day tomorrow is, they will answer, "It's Grandma's pick-up day," or "It's a stay home day," or "It's my dog's birthday."

I don't know about you, but the last time it took me 42 hours to learn something was in college as I was working towards my teaching degree. AND, these 42 hours don't take into account the calendar time these children will sit through in Kindergarten, 1st and 2nd grade.

DOI: 10.4324/9781003476719-9

I started out my preschool teaching career in a traditional preschool classroom, and I did calendar time with the children in my classes. I sat them on carpet squares, made them sit criss-cross-applesauce-hands-in-your-lap-eyes-on-me-one-two-three. I had a calendar helper who would stand at the calendar and point to the numbers as we counted them. We sang the days of the week and the months of the year and did patterns with the numbers. By *we* I mean *I* accomplished this by standing in front of the children and expecting them to retain the information I threw at them in a completely irrelevant and out-of-context method.

I spent the whole calendar time redirecting children who didn't find my circle time content exciting. I would leave at the end of every day exhausted, and with a headache, from trying to get children to do what I wanted them to do, when I wanted them to do it.

I used to think the kids were soaking up the days of the week, months, and all the math wizardry I threw at them during calendar time. Little did I know that memorization is different from understanding. It was like I was running a memorization boot camp instead of a preschool. Memorizing is not understanding.

Piaget's theory of cognitive development has shown that young children are concrete learners (more brain science stuff in a minute). Abstract thinking comes later as the brain develops— around the age of seven or eight for most children. The concepts we are hoping children learn and understand by doing calendar time are abstract. A three- to five-year-old child will have a hard time grasping a true understanding of the passage of time on a calendar. And, I can bet that most states or countries don't require a three-, four-, or five-year-old to learn calendar operations. We know they don't have a true understanding when we ask, "What day was yesterday?" and they come back with "Pajama Day!"

Three-year-olds typically "have established object permanence and can recall past events, even though they do not understand the meaning of the words 'yesterday,' 'today,' or 'tomorrow'" (CTB/McGraw-Hill 2002, 9).

> Thus, young children can talk about things that have happened or will happen, but they cannot yet understand or talk about these events in terms of units of time (days, weeks) or sequence. This child development knowledge draws into question the usefulness of calendar activities for children under age 6.
>
> (Beneke et al., 2008)

While our intentions are good, we are wasting their time with concepts that are too abstract for most young children. And who wants to spend 42 hours learning a concept they don't truly understand? They are capable of memorizing at a young age, but understanding won't come until much later when their brains are a lot more developmentally ready. Afterall, most children go through a stage where they make up words for talking about the passing of time (yesteryear and tomorrowday were some of my kids' made-up days).

Here's the brain sciencey stuff now. Stick with me; this is need-to-know information when determining if the experiences we are providing in the early childhood environment are appropriate for the children's stage of cognitive development.

Jean Piaget's theory of cognitive development has greatly influenced our understanding of how children develop their thinking abilities as they grow. According to Piaget, there are many stages of cognitive development, and each stage is marked by its own set of cognitive abilities as well as limitations. Preschool-age children are in the preoperational stage of cognitive development. Piaget found that children in the preoperational stage tend to have difficulty with abstract thinking. They are generally focused on concrete experiences and objects. Abstract concepts, such as love, time, and empathy, are often not understood and fly right over their head. In one ear and out the other, as my grandma would say. Children in the preoperational stage are more likely to think in a concrete, literal manner and thus need concrete experiences to learn and understand the world around them!

At age three, four, and five (and even two, six, and seven) children are learning about the world through their senses and concrete experiences. They may not fully grasp abstract concepts like the passing of time or "fairness" in the way that older children or adults do. Their play often revolves around concrete objects and scenarios. For example, they may engage in imaginative play with their dinosaurs and wood blocks, but their play scenarios are usually based on real-life situations they have encountered.

It is when children are around the age of seven that the concrete operational stage starts to kick in and they become more capable of abstract thinking. They can understand concepts like the passing of time and empathy for others. They are less egocentric and more capable of seeing another person's perspective. "Because of these developmental characteristics, 'it is not until the age of 7 or 8 that children have a good sense of clock time … [and] a true understanding of calendar time comes even later than that' (p. 3)" (Ethridge & King, 2005).

If we are truly wanting to do what is best practice and developmentally appropriate for young children while taking into consideration Piaget's work around cognitive development, we will break up with calendar time for good. What can we do instead to replace calendar time?

Let's think about the goals of calendar time. Is the goal to get children to learn counting and one-to-one correspondence (what they are practicing when they count the days over and over)? Is the goal to learn about the passing of time? Or maybe the goal is to get them to sit for longer periods of time so they are "ready for Kindergarten" and the long amounts of time children will have to sit still when they get to grade school. It could be that community building is the goal for calendar time.

Whatever the goal, we can find other ways to meet those goals AND the needs of the children in ways that are much more developmentally appropriate and based on classic brain research provided long ago by Dr. Piaget.

If the goal is:
Counting to 30 and one-to-one correspondence
Do this instead:
Children are natural mathematicians. They naturally want to count, sort, and classify materials in front of them.

♦ Fill your sensory table or a large tray or bin with beans (or water, sand, rice) and place gemstones, small erasers, or even rocks in the sensory table along with cups and scoops. Children will naturally want to pick out the fun extras that were added, sort them by attributes into the cups, count how many they have and compare and contrast with other children.

♦ Hide rocks with numbers 1–10 (or 20 or 30 depending on development) painted on them around the room or outdoors. Children will naturally be drawn to going on a hunt for them and then arranging them in order.

♦ Have children count how many letters are in their name. Children will naturally be curious about who has the most and who has the least amount of letters in their name.

♦ Count the children every time you transition from indoors to outdoors or vice versa. Tap their head or give them a high five as you count them. The children will naturally count with you.

If the goal is:
Learning the passing of time
Do this instead:
Young children learn about the passing of time from tangible events they have experienced in the past and things that are coming up in the future.

♦ Have a big event coming up? Make a paper chain to count down to the big thing. We used to hatch eggs each year and it took 21–23 days to incubate the eggs. We would make a countdown chain and remove one loop each day so children could see the passing of time as the chain got shorter. As the chain got shorter, the kiddos became more excited!

♦ Make a class journal. Record what you did each day with the children and include photos. Leave the journal out for children to flip through and look at the things they did in the past. This will naturally encourage talking about past events and the language that goes along with it (yesterday, last week, last summer). They may get the time labels wrong in conversation, but it shows they have a beginning understanding of the language and a natural curiosity around time.

◆ A linear calendar—use the numbers from your existing calendar chart and hide them around the classroom for children to find. For example, if it is the fifteenth of the month, hide a 15 card somewhere in the room. The rest of the numbers will already be attached to the wall (at child-accessible height) in a line. Whoever finds the 15 first will get to place it on the wall in line with the other numbers. When children see numbers in a line on the wall, they will naturally count them.

If the goal is:
Teaching children to sit for prolonged periods of time and attend to a task

Do this instead:
Young children train their bodies to sit for long periods of time by learning self-regulation. Self-regulation is not taught by sitting still, it is learned by moving their body through the environment around them. Children need to learn how their body reacts to spinning, jumping, running, rolling, climbing in order for them to learn how to rein in their body when they need to. In order for them to be able to sit still, they have to move around a lot! "Learning to sit is a process put in place by nature. And that process involves movement, which allows children to develop their proprioceptive and vestibular systems. Only when these senses have been developed will children be able to sit still" (Pica, 2021).

◆ Give children time and space where they can move their bodies as they see fit. Take on the "recess" mindset during this time and allow children to take small risks (like climbing a structure, balancing on a log, or jumping off of something).

◆ Have an obstacle course in the classroom! Let them crawl, jump, climb over and under things to learn how their bodies move through space.

◆ Provide process art experiences—gross motor style! Let them paint with brooms, mops, plungers, fly swatters, or even the wheels of a trike outdoors!

◆ Let children use too much of something. Take glue for instance, children can't learn the right amount of glue until they have used too much (or too little). And the lessons learned when having to clean up afterwards help to reinforce the lessons in self-regulation!

If the goal is:
Community building
Do this instead:
Community isn't best built through children sitting, listening, and counting together as a group. There are more effective ways of building a sense of community in an early childhood classroom.

◆ Have conversations with the children during snack and mealtimes. This is how families build their relationships, and it is a great tool for listening to one another.

◆ Turn on some music during free play and dance with the children. Joy can bring together a group faster than anything else, in my opinion!

◆ Read stories. During free play, take a seat on the couch and let children naturally gather around as you read aloud.

◆ Welcome each child as they walk in the door every single day. In the early childhood program I founded, I liked to think of it as the "Disney World Welcome." We let each child know that we were so glad to see them and that we had been eagerly waiting for them to arrive!

BUT Kristen, I love doing calendar time! I think it brings us together and the children really seem to enjoy it!

Again, from the great mind of Lisa Murphy, we need to ask ourselves three questions when contemplating the addition, continuation, or subtraction of any activity, provocation, or lesson in our early childhood environments: What am I doing? Why am I doing it? Who is it for?

> *What am I doing?* Calendar time.
> *Why am I doing it?* The goal is to help children learn to count, recognize numbers, and build community.
> *Who is it for?* You "I love doing calendar time!" (Spoiler, it should say *"The Children"* here.)

The goal should always have the children at the forefront of any decision when it comes to lesson plans, activities, and provocations. If we know children aren't capable of abstract thinking in their preschool years and we know the concept of calendar and passing of time is an abstract concept, we know the best decision is to stop doing the activity that is too abstract.

If that isn't enough to convince you, consider this information that was gathered during a circle time survey:

> Although our results suggest that calendar work and show-and-tell were the most common circle time activities, our results also show that they were not perceived by the guide as the children's favorites. In fact, our survey responses indicate that circle time activities which inspire the most interest in children (according to participants' perceptions) are often not the most frequent events of circle time. Only one of the children's preferred five activities (dance and movements) mapped to the five most frequent circle time events. Two favorites of the children, singing and music/rhythm work, were not among the 10 most frequent activities.
>
> (Koczela & Carver, 2023)

BUT Kristen, what if my administrator, program director, or co teacher insists that I do calendar time?

It is hard to change someone's mind unless they are ready to change their mind. You can feed them all the information in the world on why one way is better than another, but people hold fear around education and learning. When people are fearful, they resist. Here are a few things you can try…

1. Take advice from Lisa Murphy (The Ooey Gooey Lady) and say, "Show me what page it's on." See if the admin or the co teacher can show you where the research says calendar time is a good idea for early childhood. See if they can find what page it's on in the early learning standards book for your state or country. Does it say a three-, four-, or five-year-old needs to understand calendar operations before they get to Kindergarten? I'm guessing not.

2. Document the learning happening through play as it pertains to the administrator's perceived goal of calendar time. If their perceived goal is counting and one-to-one correspondence, take photos or videos of children counting things during play, write a caption about how they naturally counted the items, and send it off to the powers that be. (See Chapter 7 for more on observation and documentation.)

3. Show them this chapter. It's an easy read.

References

Beneke, S. J., Ostrosky, M. M., & Katz, L. G. (2008). Calendar Time for Young Children. *YC: Young Children, 63*(3), 12–16.

Ethridge, E. A., & King, J. R. (2005). Calendar Math in Preschool and Primary Classrooms. *Questioning the Curriculum. Early Childhood Education Journal, 32*(5), 291–296. https://doi.org/10.1007/s10643-005-4398-0

Koczela, A., & Carver, K. (2023). Understanding Circle Time Practices in Montessori Early Childhood Settings. *Journal of Montessori Research.* https://doi.org/10.17161/jomr.v9i2.20962

Pica, R. (2021). *What If We Taught the Way Children Learn.* Corwin Press.

9

The Pizza Parlor Heist

Ditching rotational centers and diving headfirst into free play!

Back in my traditional teaching days, in my quest to be a "real teacher" with watered down things I thought happened in Kindergarten classrooms, I wanted to create a very organized, structured "center time." I brainstormed all the ways that I could ensure that children weren't boycotting my strict rotation plan and came up with a colored clothespin system (we can't let them stay at one center too long OR skip a center). I spent a few hours one weekend with clothespins, ribbon in different colors and some very smelly glue. I made five different color clothespins (about four of each color) and introduced the concept to the children on Monday. It was pizza week. We had a pizza parlor set up in the back of the classroom and an assortment of other centers that all had a pizza theme to work on math, literacy, and crafting skills. I am sure we covered a letter P in pizza toppings I had pre-cut.

Back in the pizza parlor center, we had pizza boxes, aprons, chef hats, felt pizza and toppings, paper on clipboards for taking orders, checkered red-and-white tablecloths, and some cute little tables and chairs for the customers to use.

Before the children could dive into the centers, I explained how the clothespins worked and that they had to stay with

DOI: 10.4324/9781003476719-10

their color group and could "play" at each center until the seven-minute rotation bell rang. I had the children line up behind me, train style, with one finger in front of their lips and the other hand behind their back. They had to follow me around the room to each center so I could explain exactly what I wanted them to do at each center.

The "go" bell rang and I headed back to the pizza parlor to fulfill a childhood dream about running a restaurant. I was MADE for the job of preschool pizza parlor manager. I instructed the children to take on the roles I assigned to them. I explained what each job was and how to do it. They got about four minutes to play their assigned role because we had to rotate after seven minutes. I was having some fun, but the kids just were so whiny because they didn't want to do the job I assigned them in the pizza parlor. And then kids wanted to keep playing and wouldn't leave the center when the bell rang. What little stinkers; make up your mind!

It wasn't until after I started learning about and leaning into play that I thought back to my pizza parlor managerial position and how WILD it was that I directed their play and expected them to just drop everything after four minutes and head to the next center. No wonder I left each day with a headache and completely exhausted! No wonder I had so many situations I deemed "behavior issues" in the classroom. Children had NO autonomy. I had stripped it all from them. I was the definition of a creative vampire. I was a play robber and my heist was the pizza parlor.

Oftentimes, when an early childhood educator thinks about "centers," they think about activities set out on tables that the children must complete during a specific time of day. We think that if they complete them all and each center is a different skill (literacy, math, writing, craft, dramatic play) that we are then educating the "whole child." We are meeting each of the big domains of early learning and each child must complete each center either that day or that week in order for us to believe that we did our job and exposed the children to many activities for each of the early learning domains. Right?

It turns out centers weren't the problem in the pizza parlor, *I* was! Didactic (teacher-led) instruction is extremely limiting.

Dictating roles and time limits actually constrained the kids' capacity for authentic learning.

> Didactic instruction is presumed by many experts to inhibit intellectual development directly—by fostering superficial learning of simple responses rather than real understanding and problem-solving ability—and indirectly, by negatively affecting social-motivational variables which, in turn, affect learning-related behavior (e.g., effort, persistence). For example, experts have argued that didactic, teacher-controlled instruction that emphasizes performance undermines young children's intrinsic interest in learning (Katz, 1988), their perceptions of competence (Kamii, 1985; Katz, 1988), and their willingness to take academic risks (Elkind, 1987).
>
> (Stipek et al., 1995)

I have come to find that centers don't need their own time of day. They don't need a strict colored clothespin rotational schedule. Centers can happen any time of day, during free play. While centers are a great concept, combining them with the word "time" can have the opposite effect of what we intend. When we step away from the rigid rotational center time approach, it allows children to explore their curiosity and delve deeply into topics that captivate them.

At Butterfly Hill, a lot of thought goes into planning out the environment. The teachers plan out what will be set out on each table and anything that will be added to other areas of the classroom. Sometimes the items are built upon an interest or curiosity the children explored the previous day, and sometimes they are items/materials that are open ended so the children can play and create wherever their imagination takes them!

The "centers" in the indoor classroom included the sensory table, play dough table, art tables, manipulatives/games, the easel, dramatic play, science exploration, block area, the cozy reading area, large motor area, and a light play area. The teachers know each child won't probably make it to each area, and that is OK! Children will take what they need when they are ready and interested. They will take what they need when they are curious!

This is where observation and documentation come into play. Over time, a teacher can observe each child in play and connect what they are learning and practicing with the early learning benchmarks or standards for their area of the world. At Butterfly Hill, the teachers use a checklist for each of the Minnesota Early Childhood Indicators of Progress and check off a skill when a teacher observes a child mastering it through play! Each of the centers is carefully planned to get children curious and engaged with the materials and others around them. Over time, the teachers are able to see gaps in a child's development and can plan the environment and centers based on these findings. The teachers are detectives of learning!

I also found great joy in being sneaky about things when planning centers. One day, I put rocks with painted numbers on them in the kinetic sand table. The rocks were numbered 1–12 but I purposefully left out the 8 and the 10 rocks. I wanted to see if, through play, any children would notice some rocks were missing and if they took the time to find out what numbers were missing. Well, three kiddos fell into my learning trap that day. They were gathered around the table and called me over to tell me some rocks were missing. They had set out the rocks in order and told me 8 and 10 were missing. They worked together to count each rock, pointing at each number as they counted. I wandered away, thinking I needed a trophy for my ingenuity. A few minutes later I saw the group of little ones in the art area. I walked closer to see them using blank rocks and markers to create the number 8 and number 10 rocks. This is what a responsive child-led environment is! This kind of learning never had a chance in my pizza parlor heist days.

In educational environments that improve creative thinking, children's creative ideas are given importance and they can express their ideas freely. Children are given time to form their creative expressions. These educational environments are organised with supportive materials that allow children to have their own creative expression and make free choices (Fox and Schirrmacher 2014).

(Tok, 2022)

Centers can be a part of the everyday play environment and oftentimes don't need adult instruction for a child to figure out. If something interests a child, the learning is much more likely to stick (I call this sticky learning) than if they are forced to complete something just so we can check a box on an assessment and pat ourselves on the back.

How to Incorporate Centers

To break it down a bit more, I'll share some examples of ways to incorporate invitations/centers for children to learn in the cognitive areas of developmentally appropriate practice!

Math Concepts

Children have an innate knack for mathematics, delighting in sorting, counting, and comparing things naturally. Giving children large collections of similar items will get them to sort, compare, and count all on their own. Mathematical reasoning is an interconnected piece of the whole-child-pie. Preschoolers' willingness and ability to dive into new math concepts is correlated to their ability to play and explore.

A study done in Norway with over 1,000 toddlers found that different play skills, like interacting, being independent, pretend play, and exploring and building were connected to math skills! "Weak play skills imply weak mathematical skills, moderate play skills imply moderate mathematical skills and strong play skills imply strong mathematical skills" (Reikerås, 2020). It totally makes sense, then, to incorporate math into centers where kiddos get the chance to hone their exploring, building skills, and autonomy.

According to Ojose (2008), mastery of mathematical concepts does not come from workbooks or assignments or paper and pen. Children construct their mathematics knowledge and develop mathematical skills through hands-on experience with real-life activities. Children will use their mathematical thinking in solving actual problems in building the mathematical abilities. Children master their cognitive skills through real interactions using the various materials found in their surroundings.

(Rosli & Lin, 2018)

Here are some ideas on how to provide a mathematically rich environment that children can choose to explore in play:

- Fill the sensory table with colored pom poms, water, and containers and/or ice cube trays. The children will naturally sort the pom poms by color into the ice cube trays and containers. Add a lemon-squeezer for some extra fun. To extend this a bit further, you could use colored Sharpies or paint to make the bottom of the ice cube trays colored! Children may sort the colored pom poms into the corresponding color spot in the tray.
- Find two number puzzles that are similar but a bit different. Place the pieces all together in a basket and see if the children realize that there are two puzzles and observe them as they problem solve to figure out which pieces go to which puzzle!
- Hide the numbers 1–20 (or 30 or 10) around the room and when children find them, see what they do! You could paint them on rocks, use sticky notes, or use number magnets. Once children start to notice them, they may collect them all and maybe even put them in order!

Literacy Concepts

Many children learn their letters over time from a variety of places. It has been shown that play is a vehicle for literacy development!

Scholars have long emphasized the importance of literacy and play in early childhood education, at times examining them together (Pyle et al., 2018; Roskos & Christie, 2011). Research that addresses both the constructs of literacy and play often demonstrates the ways in which children's play supports the development of literacy skills (e.g., Barnett et al., 2008).

(Rohloff, 2022)

Early literacy learning encompasses many different things: phonics, letter recognition, letter sounds, letter formation; all of these are best developed through play!

Positive relationships between early childhood literacy rich play environments and reading and writing behaviors in the prior-to-school years can occur when adult support and appropriate literacy materials are made available to children in meaningful contexts. In this way, children are introduced to early decoding and phonics knowledge through drawing attention to letters and sounds in picture books during shared reading, letters in children's names, and dramatic play (Arrow, 2010; Christie, 2008; Mclacklan and Arrow, 2010; Piasta, 2014: Puranik and lonigan, 2012; Roskos and Christie, 2011; Roskos et at., 2010).

(Campbell, 2020)

Here are some ways to provide a literacy-rich, meaningful environment for children to learn through play:

◆ I loved to have a volunteer come into the classroom in the morning and sit on the loveseat next to the book library shelf. Children would naturally snuggle up next to the volunteer and ask them to read books all morning long. Children had the freedom to come and go as they pleased, selecting the books that piqued their interest.

◆ Place clipboards stocked with paper and bowls of small pencils all around the classroom. Children will use these organically in play to make marks, scribble, write their names or draw pictures!

- ◆ Using those same clipboards, encourage children to make a waiting list when something is popular and many children want turns! This teaches children concepts about print; top to bottom and left to right as well as problem-solving and cooperation with others!
- ◆ Use letters from old board games (Upwords, Scrabble, Bananagrams) to add to different areas of the classroom. Put them in a basket in the block area and see what children do with them. Add them to the sensory table. Children naturally look for the letters in their name and other letters that hold importance to them. When children are all playing together, they naturally learn from one another as other children find letters that are important to them and name them aloud!
- ◆ Write the children's names on slips of paper or sticky notes and hide them around the room. Children will recognize other kids' names or have conversations with others about whose name is whose!

Science Concepts

Science can be learned anywhere (just like other cognitive concepts) and oftentimes does not include the magnifying glasses or the color-mixing paddles found in many science centers in early childhood environments. Here are a few ways to incorporate science concepts into the play environment:

- ◆ Add funnels and tubes to the water table so children can use the funnels to fill up small containers with water. Add long tubing that can fit around the funnel's spout to encourage moving water to different places in the water table.
- ◆ Bring in items from outdoors for children to explore! Twigs, pinecones, shells, rocks, abandoned bird nests! Something as simple as painting rocks with water can offer really great inquiry opportunities for children!
- ◆ Place items like small catapults, prisms, or even balloon inflation pumps into the children's environment and let them explore what they do!

BUT Kristen, I have to follow a curriculum and there are centers I HAVE to do...

You can still put out the centers, but I would suggest refraining from direct teaching children how to engage with the materials (unless, of course, there are safety instructions involved or a process that needs to be followed closely). Allow children to choose if they want to engage with the centers. It *is* play if the children choose and guide their play. Leave the centers out for as long as children are still engaged in them!

When we break it down, the teachers at Butterfly Hill are planning out learning centers as they design the environment. However, they don't force children to rotate on a timed schedule and children can engage with the materials in any way they see fit!

BUT Kristen, one of the children in my class only ever wants to play with the blocks and cars. How do I get him to do any of the other centers?

Humans naturally gravitate towards what makes them comfortable. A child may be comfortable playing with the cars because that is what they play with at home. It's perfectly fine to let a child play with what makes them comfortable. Eventually, as a child gets more comfortable in the classroom, they will more than likely start to try new things. You can get a bit creative without forcing the child to do something they may not want to do. For example, if you have a kiddo who only plays with the cars, add some cars to the sensory table or paint with the wheels of a car on the easel! This can be a great creative exercise for you to think outside the box!

BUT Kristen, rotational centers are great for the kids who don't know how to play.

All mammals are born knowing how to play. Humans are born knowing how to play. It is through play that we make sense of the world. An infant plays by kicking their legs and punching their little arms in the air. A toddler plays by running and climbing on things. A preschooler may play by watching other children play or by playing with other children. Adults think play has to look like interacting with materials and other humans. This is not always the case. Mildred Parten, a prominent researcher in child development, introduced six stages of play to illustrate the various types of play children participate in as they mature and enhance their social abilities. These stages are not rigid, and children may move back and forth between them as they grow and develop social skills:

1. **Unoccupied Play:** This stage involves random movements or actions without a specific purpose or goal. This is usually seen when infants move their legs around and punch the air!

2. **Solitary (Independent) Play:** In this stage, children play alone and are focused on their own activities and interests. They typically do not interact with other children during this stage.

3. **Onlooker Play:** Children in this stage observe others playing but do not actively participate themselves. They may ask questions or make comments but do not join in the play. They watch play occur!

4. **Parallel Play:** Parallel play involves children playing alongside each other with similar items or materials, but they do not actively engage with each other. They may mimic each other's actions but do not directly interact.

5. **Associative Play:** At this stage, children start to interact with one another during play but do not necessarily have a common goal. They may share materials and engage in talk a bit to each other, but their play is still relatively unstructured without a goal in mind.

6. **Cooperative Play:** Cooperative play is the most advanced stage, where children play together in an organized manner with a common goal. They collaborate, take on different roles, and work together to achieve a shared objective. (This is the type of play most adults expect to see children doing.)

BUT Kristen, rotational centers help the children who never play with anyone to actually play with other children. I don't like when a child is left out and alone so I do rotational centers to help these kiddos out.

Our adult experiences and biases are brought into the classroom with us each day. It can be uncomfortable to see a child playing alone. There are many things to consider here about why this child is playing alone:

- ◆ The child could be overwhelmed and needs time alone to regulate.
- ◆ The child could be in the onlooker stage of play and is playing by watching others play.
- ◆ The child may not know how to ask to join into play with other children.

With those things in mind, this is another reason why it is so important to have relationships with each of the children in the classroom so you can get to know their interests, likes, dislikes, and needs. An initial reaction from an adult might be to intervene and assist the child in joining a play group. However, a deeper understanding of the child and the context fosters a more meaningful and pertinent experience for the child.

References

Campbell, S. (2020). Teaching Phonics without Teaching Phonics: Early Childhood Teachers' Reported Beliefs and Practices. *Journal of Early Childhood Literacy*, *20*(4): 783–814.

Reikerås, E. (2020). Relations between Play Skills and Mathematical Skills in Toddlers. *ZDM*, *52*(4), 703–716. https://doi.org/10.1007/ss11858-020-01141-1

Rohloff, R. (2022). The Intersection of Literacy and Play in Early Childhood: A Systematic Review of the Literature. *Proceedings of the 2022 AERA Annual Meeting.* https://doi.org/10.3102/1893702

Rosli, R., & Lin, T. W. (2018). Children Early Mathematics Development Based on a Free Play Activity. *Creative Education*, 9, 1174–1185.

Tok, E. (2022). Early Childhood Teachers' Roles in Fostering Creativity through Free Play. *International Journal of Early Years Education*, *30*(4), 956–968. https://doi.org/10.1080/09669760.2021.1933919

10

The Eagle That Taught Literacy Skills

Letters don't need a week; they're more meaningful when we weave them into what excites kids and sparks their curiosity!

Back in my traditional teacher days, we did a letter every week. We didn't have a rhyme or reason for what letters we picked to teach for which week, so we tried to blend the letter of the week with the theme of the week. P was for Pizza week. I instructed the children to make large letter Ps with pizza toppings crafted to the top, play pizza parlor in the dramatic play area, sing "I am a Pizza," and play circle time games that reinforced the letter P.

A was for alligator and children made large chomping alligators shaped like the letter A. D was for Dot so the children wore dots to school and used bingo daubers to decorate a letter D to take home (a receipt that said, "Hey look, I taught your child the letter D today!"). It felt good to be organized and ensure that we got all the letters conquered throughout the school year!

In my play-based program, we didn't do a letter each week. I read a book called *No More Letter of the Week* by Patricia D.

DOI: 10.4324/9781003476719-11

Lusche (2003) and it changed the way I looked at literacy instruction in early childhood. I realized that children learn letters best when they're connected to something meaningful to them (and that often doesn't happen on a weekly schedule).

In her book, *The Whole Child Alphabet: How Young Children Actually Develop Literacy*, Stacey Benge (2023) writes,

> If there is no letter of the week, how do we teach the alphabet? [Data and research] indicate that, when it comes to classroom practice, (1) not every letter requires the same instructional attention; (2) whole-class instruction focused on a particular letter is inefficient …: (3) no one sequence for teaching letters and their associated sounds is optimal for all children" (McKay & Teale, 2015). This is wonderful news because it frees us from the constraints of only one letter at a time.

I witnessed this first-hand in the preschool classroom!

I had a child in my class at Butterfly Hill who was a math wizard. Lo was able to add and subtract two- and three-digit numbers by doing mental math. One day, I created a 100s chart on posterboard for him and a few other kiddos at Butterfly Hill who were really into numbers and number order. I wrote the numbers 1–100 on poker chips and placed them in a basket next to the chart and left them on the table for them to find one morning. They conquered that 100s chart like 1st graders without any instruction from an adult!

Lo loved all things numbers, but seemed to have an aversion for letters (except those in his own name). He would bypass our morning check-in if it included letter recognition or writing letters. Lo preferred not to pick up a pencil to write anything (unless it was a number) and spent a lot of his time in very active rough and tumble play and fantasy play.

One evening I was scrolling social media and saw that the Department of Natural Resources in Minnesota had a live camera feed on an eagle's nest. I tuned in to the live feed and saw a pair of bald eagles nestled in a gigantic nest. They were covered in snow. The female eagle was sitting on two eggs that she had recently laid in the past three days. I was invested in this eagle pair's love story and became so fascinated with the video feed that I kept it up on my laptop in the classroom during the day. Of course children were intrigued with this, as I never had any sort of screen out for the children to use or watch. Children naturally started asking a ton of questions about the eagles. I told them the story of the two eagles and the two eggs. "How long until the eggs hatch?" "What will the baby eagles look like?" "Which one is the dad bird and which is the mom bird?"

Lo was one of the kiddos gathered around the laptop screen that morning. He was a silent onlooker but I could tell he was curious and intrigued with the eagles. After everyone cleared away and the excitement had died down, I found Lo watching the eagles all by himself. His friends were off playing, and he was drawn in to the eagles' nest. I wandered over to watch along with him. There was only one bird in the nest at that time. Being a hummingbird teacher (explained in Chapter 4), I sat quietly and waited for him to say something if he felt like it. He said, "They are beautiful." "I know!" I responded. He was silent for a bit longer and then said, "I wonder if they are cold." I replied by explaining they have feathers that act like a winter jacket. He watched the eagles for a bit longer and all of a sudden one of the eagles came swooping back into the nest. It perched on the side while the other eagle carefully got up and moved off the eggs. Lo gasped when he saw the two eggs and watched in awe as the other eagle took its place on top of the eggs.

Lo left me alone at the computer and ran across the room to grab his journal. The majority of pages in his journal were empty, save for sporadic scribbles and occasional sketches of numbers scattered throughout. He grabbed a small golf size pencil from a bowl on the shelf and hurried back over to me. He opened up the journal and asked me if I could help him write the word EAGLE in his journal. I guided him through the formation of each letter while he wrote the letters at the top of a page. Then he asked, "How long until the baby eagles hatch?" I didn't know, so we did some googling and found that it takes 35 days for an eagle egg to incubate. He started to list all of the numbers 1–35 on the journal page. Then he looked up at me and asked, "How do you spell BABY CHICK?" He wrote those words on the bottom of the page as I guided him through the formation of each of those letters. He told me that he was going to cross off a number each day until they hatched!

The next day he came running into school with a larger version of his countdown checklist. His parent mentioned that he had dedicated time and effort to it after school. They also asked if I had taught him how to spell, as Lo had independently written the words "eagle," "baby," and "chick."

Holy crap! I knew (because of play research) that children will learn best when they are curious and interested in something and when it has meaning to them. Lo was SO curious about these eagles that suddenly the letters held meaning. He needed that meaning to organize the letters in his brain. The quick moment I took to help him spell the words stuck. He learned ten letters that day. That is almost half of the letters in the alphabet. Pair that with his own name and he could recognize and write 15 letters!

This little guy with zero interest in letters gave me a lesson in child-led, inquiry-based learning that day. Letters don't need a week. They just need curiosity and meaning. And each child's meaning comes at different times.

Why is Letter of the Week a standard practice in many early childhood programs? Well, it could be because children haven't been exposed to a more effective practice or because it simplifies the overwhelming task and responsibility of teaching children the foundational skills of literacy. Sure, craft projects like the P for Pizza and D for Dot provide children a way to connect literacy to hand-on experiences; but are they actually connecting any deeper meaning to the letters? (McKay & Teale 2015).

Young children learn the alphabet and letter sounds most effectively through play-based, organic, and interest-driven methods rather than through didactic instruction and rote memorization (the teacher talking more than the children). Play offers children opportunities to engage with letters in ways that are meaningful to them. When things are meaningful, learning sticks (meaning children get a deeper understanding and retain the info)! When children play, they naturally explore and experiment with language, discovering the shapes, sounds, and meanings of letters in ways that hold personal meaning!

Benge (2023) writes,

> The concept of alphabet knowledge needs to go beyond just naming letters and their sounds …. Move past the lesson plans dictated by purchasing curriculums that focus on a preset list of outcomes. Leave behind activities that revolve around letter of the week, flash cards, and worksheets as these tend to skip steps and just "surface teach."

Print-Rich Environments

So, how can we ensure that children are exposed to letters during play? One effective way children learn the alphabet through play is through print-rich environments. In a thoughtfully set up play environment, letters/words/sounds are integrated throughout the day. Felt letters adorn the felt board, magnetic letters cling to the refrigerator, clipboards and golf pencils are scattered around the classroom for children to use in creating marks, letters, shapes, or words on paper. There are also reading books, alphabet blocks for play, and various opportunities for artistic expression. Children encounter letters in various ways throughout the day, allowing them to make connections between letters and maybe even their corresponding sounds. When a child is playing in the sensory table filled with magnetic letters and magnet wands, they may notice the first letter of their name and begin to associate that letter with the sound it represents!

Multisensory Experiences

Another way to enhance alphabet learning and retention is through play-based environments that often involve multisensory experiences. Bev Bos, a play-based learning advocate, was quoted as saying, "The basics for young children are wonder, discovery and experience. If it hasn't been in the hand, the body and the heart, it can't be in the brain." When children engage in hands-on activities like tracing letters in sand, stamping letters in play dough, singing songs, writing in their journal, or creating art, they utilize multiple senses, reinforcing their understanding of letter shapes and sounds. These multisensory experiences create stronger neural connections in the brain, leading to sticky learning.

Organic and inquiry-based methods of introducing letters to children capitalize on their intrinsic motivation and curiosity (like Lo and the eagles). When children have the opportunity to explore letters in ways that match their interests and preferences, they become active participants in their own learning journey. This engagement was evident when Lo sought help writing "eagle," "baby," and "chick," taking initiative and showing deep engagement. A personalized approach not only enriched his experience but also fostered a strong sense of ownership!

If I had insisted that every child "learn" the letters in the words "eagle" and "baby chick," only a few children would likely have connected meaningfully with those letters and words. Some kids couldn't care less about an eagle and its eggs. This didactic instruction and memorization of letters often lacks context and relevance for some children. Rote repetition of letter names and sounds without meaningful connections may lead to shallow understanding and limited retention. Children who don't care about eagles and baby chicks may struggle to transfer their memorized knowledge to real-world situations because they lack a deeper understanding of how these letters function within language.

BUT Kristen, I am required to teach letter of the week, is there a way around it?

First, I'd ask for a definition of what the "letter of the week" teaching method entails. Does it mean direct instruction? If so, you could incorporate this into a morning check-in activity as children come in the door before they start playing.

Does it mean giving children the opportunity to practice the letter each day? If that's the case, integrate this into the environment by setting up the activity on a table, allowing children to choose whether they want to participate or not. Get a bit creative and think outside the box. Oftentimes curricula or administrative requirements don't force you to stand in front and teach about the letter, so you can get creative and introduce it in different ways!

BUT Kristen, what if they don't know all of their letters and sounds by the time they go to Kindergarten?

We don't get all bent out of shape if a baby doesn't walk by ten months. Nope, we trust they will start walking when they are ready. We all know that some babies walk at nine months and some at 14 months. The same is true for academic knowledge. Some children will know more letters and numbers than others and that is OK! If you have concerns about how many letters or numbers a child "should" know before they enter Kindergarten, it is best to check out your state or country standards to see what is suggested as a target! I suggest this with a small caveat, as some states have standards that are much more developmentally appropriate than others. And remember, knowing the letters of the alphabet and numbers is such a SMALL part of the whole-child-pie. We can't forget about all of the other areas of whole child development and how important those are!

BUT Kristen, I have been doing "letter of the week" for years and have all my lesson plans for this.

When we know better, we can do better. If you now know that many of the activities that go along with "letter of the week" aren't the most developmentally appropriate way to teach letters, then you can get excited about doing some new and different things in your classroom. Afterall, preschool is about the child. Not about you.

BUT Kristen, the children love letter of the week.

Do they? Or is that all they know? I can bet that if you scrapped letter of the week and let children play a little longer, they wouldn't miss it. Educators often cite this as a reason to retain elements that may not be developmentally appropriate in their classrooms, out of concern for losing control or disrupting established practices. I encourage you to do an experiment for a couple of weeks. You can still offer your letter of the week activities, but do it during playtime. See how many children actually LOVE it and choose to do those activities. However, it's essential to provide children with opportunities to explore other materials concurrently. The experiment wouldn't yield fair results if only "letter of the week" activities were available.

References

Benge, S. (2023). *The Whole Child Alphabet: How Young Children Actually Develop Literacy*. Exchange Press.

Lusche, P. D. (2003). *No More Letter of the Week: A Framework for Integrating Reading Strategies and Cueing Systems with Letter-Sound Introduction*. Staff Development for Educators.

McKay, R., & Teale, W. H. (2015). *No More Teaching Letter A Week*. Portsmouth: Heinemann.

11

Circle Time Anarchy

Long circle times are inappropriate, counterproductive, and boring.

I'm embarrassed to admit that this occurred a few years into my play-based learning journey. During that time, I still carried some unchecked ego to the circle time carpet, feeling the need to control the children. As a result, all of the children boycotted my circle time. Here's what unfolded…

I had planned a "fun" circle time. I hadn't really taken into consideration the children's interests at this point, and I planned something that *I* thought would be engaging. Despite understanding that children learn through movement and that circle times should not focus on sitting still, I designed a sedentary circle time that lacked engagement. *Can you guess where this is going?* The children were bored, fidgeting, bothering each other, and simply not interested in what I had planned for them. I told the group that if they didn't want to be at circle time, they could go back to the couch and sit quietly and look at books or choose a puzzle. EVERYONE LEFT. I didn't try to get them back, but the control part of me thought, "I'll get them."

The next day I planned the most engaging circle time of all. A BUBBLEGUM TASTE TESTING CIRCLE TIME. And I set them up.

DOI: 10.4324/9781003476719-12

I said, "If you don't feel like being at circle time, you can always choose to go look at books or do a puzzle quietly while we do stories and games on the rug!" I had two kids left who were going to get to taste all the bubblegum! When I pulled out the bubblegum and proclaimed loudly for all to hear that we were going to taste them all, all of the kids came running back. But, my ego was there and I felt the urge to control. So I told the kids who left that they couldn't come back. "You chose to leave so you can't come back to circle time." They had to watch from the other side of the classroom as we ate bubblegum. It actually makes me queasy to think that I did this. I try to remind myself that I didn't have the understanding I do now, and I was doing my best, but it still makes me sad to think about it.

Circle time is generally used in traditional preschool environments as a way to "play teacher," so that it looks like we are "teaching" and filling the children's brains with all the things. I ran a very conventional circle time when I was in my traditional preschool teaching days. I had carpet squares that I would meticulously arrange so that children wouldn't bother each other. The children were all to sit criss-cross applesauce with their hands in their laps. I had the weather helper and the calendar helper and the carpet helper. We sang our days of the week song, months of the year song, and weather song. We did "Today is Monday, yesterday was Sunday, and tomorrow is Tuesday" chant with no one ever getting the days correct. Then the calendar helper would stand next to the calendar and we would count all the days as they moved the pointer. They often got so bored the pointer would slip and I would have to jump up and put the pointer back on the correct number. AND THEN. And then we did the pattern. On the number cards in most calendar sets, you can choose different scenes for the month you are in. For instance, if it was October, we used the leaf and pumpkin cards. Pumpkin, Pumpkin, Leaf. Pumpkin, Pumpkin, _____? The children guessed the next picture for the pattern. It took a considerable amount of time, making it a challenge to keep them all sitting in a cross-legged position and focused either on me or the calendar.

Top this off with teacher-directed centers, table time, and little to no outdoor play and it is a recipe for disaster. Meaning, adults won't attain the level of control they're seeking, and children won't have their developmental needs met. Disaster for both parties involved.

After gaining more classroom experience, observing children during playtime, and expanding my knowledge on how children learn through play, I came to understand that they required a different approach from what I was offering during circle time. They needed movement, developmentally appropriate content, stories to engage their imagination and curiosity and maybe some singing and/or fingerplays. They didn't need direct instruction on a topic. They didn't need calendar time (lots more about this in Chapter 8). They didn't need weather time. They didn't need show-and-tell. They didn't need an adult telling them to sit criss-cross applesauce. They needed a supportive adult who is developmentally informed to lead them in an engaging and brief time in the day to build a sense of community.

There was a massive study done called the IEA Preprimary Project that has proven children will perform better academically at age seven if they had less "schoolified," whole group experiences at age four:

> Using hierarchical linear modeling at the levels of the child, setting type, and country, the analysis showed, among other things, that children had better language and cognitive performance at age 7 if their age 4 settings emphasized free-choice activities and if their teachers had more teacher education. Furthermore, children had better cognitive performance if they spent less time in whole-group activities and had access to a greater number and variety of materials ([28], p. 77).
>
> (Hayes, 2008)

The same study shows that children need *less* whole group instruction and *more* variety of materials to learn and exercise creativity!

> Learning and creativity grow when situations pique children's interest and stretch their imaginations. By definition, activities for the whole group—with the exception

of free play— are not tailored to an individual child's interest or learning ability. To build cognitive skills, young children need to solve problems and explore materials on their own. In settings with an inadequate number or variety of materials, children do not have as many opportunities to experiment and solve problems at their own pace.

(Montie et al., 2007)

This study underscores the significance of early childhood education practices that promote individualized learning, creativity, and problem-solving. By emphasizing free-choice activities, providing diverse materials, and minimizing whole-group instruction, educators can better support cognitive development and academic success for their students. These findings highlight the need for educational environments that cater to children's interests (turkey hunts!), encourage exploration ("Is that turkey poop?"), and foster a love for learning (inspecting and cutting a real live turkey feather) from a young age. Circle time does little to promote these individualized needs!

But, do they actually neeeeeed a circle time at all? If we back things up a bit and question where the whole ritual of circle time began, maybe we just do it because it has always been done. Circle time isn't "bad," and it can exist in a developmentally appropriate way.

At Butterfly Hill, circle time is used as a transition time between indoor play and outdoor play. It gives some of the adults in the space time to tidy things up and get gear ready to take outdoors. Circle time is very brief—about 10–15 minutes—and includes songs and movement, a read-aloud or oral story and maybe a short game if time allows, and children are engaged. It is more of a transitional group time than a traditional circle time. Circle time should not be seen as the end all be all for learning in the classroom, physically or cognitively!

BUT Kristen, I use circle time to help children practice sitting for long periods of time so they can sit for long periods of time in Kindergarten.

Children don't learn to sit still by sitting still. Rae Pica (2021) writes, "Can you imagine if we insisted that kittens, puppies, and baby goats stay still? If we prevented them from frolicking and playing? The idea is ludicrous—and it should be just as ludicrous when we're discussing children."

How about this gold from, yet again, Rae Pica (2021):

> We treat children as though they exist only from the neck up and only their brains matter, when the research shows and good sense validates the importance of the mind–body connection. The failure to acknowledge this connection is the primary reason why play and movement are eliminated from early childhood classrooms—and why young children are forced to sit for long periods. And what sense does that make when research has also demonstrated that sitting increases fatigue and reduces concentration?

Pica also suggests that "Learning to sit is a *process* put in place by nature. And that process involves *movement*, which allows children to develop their proprioceptive and vestibular systems. Only when these senses have been developed will children be able to sit still."

Children need to MOVE to learn! Their bodies need practice running, jumping, spinning, and climbing in order for them to develop the skills necessary for sitting for long periods of time!

> When educating teachers and parents about children's sitting behaviour, I start by highlighting the importance of children being actively involved in gross motor activities (i.e. crawling, climbing, jumping, running, etc.) at home and in early childhood classrooms, before participating in seated learning activities.
>
> (Papworth, 2020)

Here is some great research to consider when getting children to sit for long periods for circle time:

> Research indicates that lengthy circle gatherings result in adverse outcomes. In a study of 122 four and five year old

children, the long duration of circle time (sometimes up to 30–40 minutes) was directly associated with negative reactions in children (Wiltz & Klein, 2001). Another study (Bustamante et al., 2018) found that circle time engagement decreased if it lasted more than 20 minutes; at the beginning of circle time, child engagement was generally high, but it declined in all classrooms as time progressed. Half of the classrooms had significant disengagement, with over 30% of students off task.

(Koczela & Carver, 2023)

BUT Kristen, if I let children sit however they want at circle time, they will all lay down or stand up and bug each other.

I was the criss-cross-applesauce-eyes-on-me-one-two-three-hands-in-your-lap-marshamllow-in-your-mouth preschool teacher. I believed that children needed to sit in a cross-legged position to focus on the information I was attempting to teach to them. Little did I know that forcing children to sit a certain way can actually do the opposite of what I was trying to accomplish. Forcing a child to sit a certain way could be a challenging thing for them and so their attention may be used up trying to comply with an uncomfortable sitting position. This means they are less likely to be paying attention and more likely to be bothering the child seated next to them.

When circle time content is developmentally appropriate and engaging, children will forget about bothering the child next to them. If they have a patient and supportive teacher who understands child development and the movement needs of children, it really doesn't take long for children to organize themselves on a rug in a position that is comfy for their body.

If we look at the anatomy of the spine and the body, the body benefits mostly from engaging in activities which encourage movement as much as possible, or resting in a tummy-time position. Other positions that the anatomy of the body would prefer include: sitting with the legs stretched out straight in front, walking while having a group session (similar to a tour-guide session), standing with both feet evenly on the ground while singing/ listening, varying the seated position every six to seven minutes so that the body receives the circulation and movement that it needs.

(Papworth, 2020)

When I held circle times, I allowed children to lay down, stand up, sit on a chair or on the rug in a position that was comfortable to them. I would guide children who wanted to stand to the back so that the children in front could still see. The children who wanted to lay down were allowed to do so on the side so as not to bother other children with their arms or legs. The children who wanted to sit in a chair could do so in front of the standing children. We never really made an actual circle as I knew that, when reading, the closer children are to the teacher, the more engaged they are!

> First, students seated close to the book and teacher were more engaged. The close children had a clearer view of the images, which convey meaning, and, therefore, they may have been able to contribute in more meaningful ways to the story reading and discussion. The closeness may have resulted in their feeling more connected to the teacher and, thus, the activity the teacher was promoting.
>
> (Paciga et al., 2022)

BUT Kristen, I use circle time as a chance to check for skills the children need to learn so I can check off that they learned it on my assessment tool.

I came up with a great idea many years ago that is still used at Butterfly Hill. It's a time to check for understanding in a developmentally appropriate manner and at an appropriate time in the classroom. I call it Morning Check-In (so creative, I know) and it is done every morning when children arrive. After they have hung up their backpack and taken off their jacket, the children come to the check-in table that is positioned by the door.

It is important to note that morning check-in is completely voluntary and children don't have to participate if they don't want to! Because the activities presented are quick, engaging, and developmentally appropriate, most children decide to participate. There are some days when a child or two doesn't wish to participate and that is OK!

Morning check-in is used to connect one-on-one with each student each day, provide direct instruction on an activity that needs instructions (like using a real hammer and nail), or as a check for understanding on a benchmark that we have not seen most children meet during free play (for example, hopping on one foot). We can then check off the benchmark if we see they have mastered it!

Each child has either a rock or a tree cookie (a slice of a tree branch) with their name on it. Sometimes they find their name and use their name to complete the check-in. For example, ask the children how many pockets they are wearing. They must count their pockets and then put their rock/tree cookie in the bowl with the corresponding number. We get to see if they can count one-to-one correspondence and we get to see if they can recognize the number by the bowl.

Sometimes the children don't need their rock for the question or task so they just locate their name rock and place it in the bowl, letting us know they are at school. Then we have them do an activity that involves a few steps. Maybe they must roll a die, count the spots, and then jump that many times on one foot. We can check for following multi-step directions, one-to-one correspondence, and if they are able to balance and hop on one foot.

We also differentiate the activity based on the development of each child. Let's say we have the table-top whiteboard filled with uppercase letters drawn in dry erase marker. We may have children who are unfamiliar with letters choose a letter from a bag and find that matching letter on the board and erase it with their finger. We can tell them verbally what the letter is while they look for the match: "You found the letter M! Mom starts with letter M!" Another child may know a lot of letters, so we verbally tell them to find the letter M and erase it. A child who is familiar with most letters and is curious about letter sounds may be able to find the letter based on a sound. We say, "Find the letter that makes the 'mmm sound for mom' and erase it."

Sometimes we want to show children a new process they haven't done before like hammering a nail with a real hammer. We want to teach them the safety behind tool use, so we have the table stocked with safety glasses, a pumpkin, nails or golf tees, and a real hammer. We can walk them through how to tap lightly to get the nail into the pumpkin.

All of the things that show up on an assessment can be checked over the course of time through morning check-in. It takes a bit of planning and creativity on the part of the adults, but presenting information in an engaging and playful manner is far more developmentally suitable than interrupting children's play for formal assessments.

References

Hayes, N. (2008). Teaching Matters in Early Educational Practice: The Case for a Nurturing Pedagogy. *Early Education & Development*, *19*(3), 430–440. https://doi.org/10.1080/10409280802065395

Koczela, A., & Carver, K. (2023). Understanding Circle Time Practices in Montessori Early Childhood Settings. *Journal of Montessori Research*. https://doi.org/10.17161/jomr.v9i2.20962

Montie, J. E., Claxton, J., & Lockhart, S. D. (2007). A Multinational Study Supports Child-Initiated Learning: Using the Findings in Your Classroom. *YC: Young Children*, *62*(6), 22–26.

Paciga, K. A., Lisy, J. G., Teale, W. H., & Hoffman, J. L. (2022). Student Engagement in Classroom Read-Alouds: Considering Seating and Timing. *Illinois Reading Council Journal*, *50*(4), 38–46. https://doi.org/10.33600/IRCJ.50.4.2022.38

Papworth, R. (2020). Children Sitting During Circle Time at Kindergarten: From an Exercise Physiology Perspective. *Educating Young Children: Learning & Teaching in the Early Childhood Years*, *26*(3), 8–12.

Pica, R. (2021). *What If We Taught the Way Children Learn*. Corwin Press.

12

Behavior Charts in the Teacher's Lounge

Punishments and rewards miss the whole point; they are band aids and quick fixes.

Imagine this: As you enter the new school year, the director or principal introduces a new system to ensure that everyone is doing their job. She has all of your names on clothespins and they are placed on a chart on the wall in the teacher's lounge. When she thinks that you are doing what you should be doing, your clothespin stays on green (for good work!). Let's say you wake up to some really bad news one day, which makes you a bit late for work and you are mentally distracted throughout the day. Your boss decides that you aren't doing your best work. She moves your clothespin down to yellow (which means "think about it"). You see it in the break room and can feel other teachers looking at you because you are the only one on yellow that day. Your day continues to go downhill and you can't stop thinking about your clothespin that's parked on the yellow section. The next day you show up with a fresh outlook on life, until you see your clothespin still on yellow. No one even talked to you about it. You're immediately upset. Everyone can see it and you shut down even more. The boss lowers your clothespin to red (for "see me in my office"). You are now the talk of the break room and your spirit is broken. You have no trust in your boss, you're wary of your colleagues, and you wish you could quit!

Doesn't that sound horrible?! This happens every day in classrooms and early childhood programs! And truth be told, I did a form of this. Before I knew better.

Before I knew better, I read children a book about being a bucket filler (a pretty abstract concept for a four-year-old to grasp). When I saw children being bucket fillers, I would write their name on a slip of paper and put it in a bucket that I had made on a really cute bulletin board. Once we got the bucket filled, I had some class reward planned. I want to barf thinking about this. The worst part? If I saw them being a "hole in the bucket" (meaning they weren't acting in a way towards others that I thought they should be acting), I took their name out of the bucket. So gross!

This happens more than we know in classrooms everywhere. Rewards and punishments used as a way to control the behavior of children.

My own son was dreading running the mile in PE class because it was timed, and it felt like too much pressure, ruining all the fun. He mentioned that the gym teacher was giving out popsicles to the whole class if they could all show improvement in their time from running the mile earlier in the year. Fast forward a few weeks and he was sick the day everyone else ran the mile. He found out that five kids didn't show improvement and so no popsicles were to be had. He didn't care what his time was because he wasn't getting a popsicle anyway. And he went on to let me know which five kids didn't improve and "ruined" it for the whole class. I WAS THE NON-ATHLETIC KID WHO THOUGHT I WAS DYING WHEN I RAN THE MILE IN GRADE SCHOOL. I was always one of the last ones to cross the finish line. If that wasn't mortifying enough, the threat of ruining a popsicle reward for the whole class would have had me pooping my pants while I was running. Imagine being one of the children who didn't show improvement and now everyone knows they don't get a popsicle because of you. How mortifying. This is NOT how children should be treated.

When you walk down the hallway with a coworker, do you walk in complete silence? Probably not. When my daughter was in 4th grade, her teacher made them line up and walk through the halls completely quietly. If they made any noise, they had to turn around and do it again. One day, they missed the first half of music class because the teacher wasn't satisfied with the way they walked in the hallway. They had to walk it six times. Sidenote: I posted about this on social media and got a call from the principal asking me to take it down and apologize to the teacher. UMMMMMMM, don't do things like that to children if you are embarrassed about it or know that children shouldn't be treated this way. Can you tell that this subject fires me up?

I recently came across a video of an early childhood educator filming themselves trying to get some children to stop crying. The children were about three years old and were seated on the rug, crying. They had had recess taken away from them for "not listening." A teacher was trying to reason with them, letting them know that they need to listen in order to go to recess next time. Three-year-olds don't listen for many reasons; they aren't trying to be bad! There are so many reasons a child may not be listening (or displaying any other behavior an adult labels as "misbehaving"). A three-year-old may not listen because they aren't in a developmentally appropriate environment. The child may have needs that aren't being met, and the adults around them don't understand that a child can't listen if they have an itchy butt! If we can be detectives and get to the root of the behavior that is seen as a "misbehavior" in the eyes of the adult, then we can better serve the children in our care without using coercion and manipulation techniques to get them to behave in a way that we see as "good."

A not so sidenote: RECESS SHOULD NEVER BE TAKEN AWAY FROM A CHILD.

When I travel to conferences, schools, and child care programs to speak and teach them about play and child-centered learning, I have the adults list all of the things that children do that they say "no" to frequently or things that drive them bananas. The lists are always pages long and include things like hitting, kicking, biting, spitting, whining, crying, noodling (when a child throws a tantrum and flops their body to the ground so you can't pick them up), not listening, running inside, climbing on things, dumping out toys and not playing with them, throwing things, breaking toys, knocking other children's block towers over, throwing sand, dumping things out of the sensory table, picking their nose, using too much glue, going up the slide, licking things, hands in their pants, not sharing, taking things from others, saying potty words or bad words, and the list could go on.

Every single thing listed is 100 percent developmentally appropriate for the age group of children with whom we are working. It's just inconvenient for the adults in the room. "We have teaching to do." "We can't deal with all these behaviors all the time." So rewards and punishments get used to coerce children to act in a way that is convenient for the adults. We forget that understanding children and coaching them through these behaviors *is* teaching.

While I do not admit to being an expert when it comes to behavior, rewards, and punishments, I do believe that children are doing the best they can. And adult caregivers are as well. But if you find yourself reading this chapter and thinking a bit more deeply about this topic, keep going. Keep learning. I still am, and it is a daily decision to show up and keep learning for the children in my life.

What if early childhood educators that are stuck in the "misbehavior" mindset could shift their thinking a little bit and realize that a huge part of early childhood education is helping children to work through things? What if we realized that many of the behaviors deemed "bad" by adults are simply children's way of expressing unmet needs? What if we could realize that perhaps our expectations aren't developmentally appropriate? The cool thing is that in play-based environments, teachers DO have time to help with all of the things children are testing out. All of the ways they are using trial and error to learn about the world around them. That is the magic in play. When adults have enough information to understand that children aren't intentionally "bad," but are instead trying to make sense of the world and express their unmet needs, they can respond effectively to each child and watch the "misbehaviors" begin to dissipate.

Here is something to ponder… If you have ever worked with an infant before, there is a mental checklist that adults go through in their head when the baby cries. Are they wet, tired, hot/cold, hurt, need a cuddle, scared, hungry, overwhelmed? But as soon as a child can say a few sentences and walk, we instantly think they are monsters out to get us when they whine and cry. We forget that they still have all the same needs as an infant, and they probably don't have any idea why they are crying. Heck, I'm 43 and cry sometimes without knowing why. That infant checklist? It closely aligns with Maslow's Hierarchy of Needs!

If you are not familiar with Maslow's Hierarchy of Needs, Abraham Maslow (1943) suggested a psychological theory that human needs can be categorized into a hierarchical structure, with basic physiological needs at the bottom and higher-order needs at the top. At the base are the most basic needs for life: air, water, food, shelter, and sleep. These are known as physiological needs. The second level is safety needs: safety and security, stability, and financial security. The third level involves social needs, which include the need for love, belongingness, and meaningful connections with others. Above that are esteem needs, which are the desire for self-esteem, respect from others, recognition, and a sense of accomplishment. At the very top of the hierarchy is self-actualization, which is the fulfillment of one's potential, pursuit of personal growth, creativity, and the desire for meaning and purpose in life. The top level represents curiosity and learning.

Maslow proposed that each of the lower levels must be met in order for the higher levels to be reached. So, if a child is hungry, they can't be curious and learning can't happen. If a child has an itchy butt, they can't learn. If a child doesn't feel a connection with any of the adults in the room, learning won't happen. Children show us their needs aren't being met by doing things that adults deem "misbehaviors."

Nel Noddings, prominent educator and philosopher, really hammered home the idea of Caring Education. She emphasized the importance of fostering caring relationships between teachers and students. It's not just about lesson plans and assessments; it's about empathy, understanding, and showing mutual respect in the classroom. She was all for creating an environment where students feel interconnected within a supportive educational community. Kiddos simply cannot learn well if they don't feel cared for and appreciated (Zhang & Zheng, 2021)!

Take what we know about Caring Education and the understanding of human needs. Add in behavior charts, threaten "no recess" punishments for being too loud or active, and dangle "all class popsicle rewards" for running the mile in ten minutes or less; we are doing more harm than good. We're sacrificing long-term mental health for short-term behavior compliance.

> If a teacher needs [a behavior chart] at all, if they have this hanging on their wall, they're not *managing* behavior, they're threatening it by holding a child's reputation hostage. They're trying to make the negative behaviors go away because they're too routined with this lazy technique and too steadfast in their control to actually deal with them in a developmentally appropriate way. They're telling kids: the most important reason to meet my requirements of you is because you need to care about what the teacher and all of your friends think of you.
>
> (Manley, 2015)

There are many reasons why we are seeing more challenging behaviors in early childhood settings: Not enough play, inappropriate expectations for the age and stage children are in, not enough downtime and stifling creativity with didactic teaching techniques are some of the reasons why children show behaviors that adults deem "bad" (Pica, 2021). This feels like more of a "teacher" problem and less of a "kids being kids" problem.

I promise, if you let children play, the behaviors that pop up are developmentally appropriate and the adults and children are all much happier! AND when we change our mindset to social/emotional coach instead of judge and jury, we can help children develop skills that better prepare them to meet the expectations when they enter elementary school. Teaching in early childhood should include teaching children how to work through emotions, dysregulation, and tough social situations with other children in the classroom.

Let's take some time to look at punishments and rewards (two very popular behavior management techniques used in early childhood programs) and the reasons that these techniques can be detrimental to the children. Alfie Kohn (2010) writes, "The troubling truth is that *rewards and punishments are not opposites at all; they are two sides of the same coin.* And it is a coin that does not buy very much."

Rewards

Extrinsic rewards like stickers or treats (or in my case bucket-filing sticky notes), do the exact opposite of what we are hopeful for over time:

♦ **Lowered Intrinsic Motivation:** Research suggests that extrinsic rewards can diminish intrinsic motivation! When children are rewarded for playing or learning, they might begin to pursue these activities solely for rewards rather than actually enjoying doing the thing. If learning loses its joy, a child may start to view it as a chore! "It has been shown that 20-month-old infants already are less likely to engage in further helping if they have received a material reward in a previous treatment phase as compared to infants who received praise or no reward at all (Warneken & Tomasello, 2008). These findings support the claim that even the earliest altruistic acts like helping behavior in young children are intrinsically motivated rather than socialized via material rewards" (Ulber et al., 2016).

♦ **Dependency on Rewards:** If children get m&ms every time they poop on the toilet instead of in their diaper, that child may come to expect m&ms every time they have to poop. If you run out of m&ms, you may well be changing a diaper again. Relying on a reward lessens their ability to appreciate doing something for its own sake. Children may lose interest in an activity once the reward is no longer offered, which, in a preschool setting, can diminish long-term engagement and curiosity. "In a seminal study of the overjustification effect in children, Lepper et al. (1973) investigated preschoolers' intrinsic motivation to perform a drawing task. Children were assigned to one of the three conditions in which they (a) expected a reward for performing the task, (b) received a reward unexpectedly afterward, or (c) neither expected nor received a reward. Only children who expected and eventually obtained a reward were less motivated to continue drawing afterward. Crucially, children's intrinsic interest in drawing remained stable and did not differ between conditions in which subjects received an unexpected reward or no reward at all" (Ulber et al., 2016).

◆ **Impact on Risk-Taking and Creativity:** Extrinsic rewards can lead children to choose easier tasks so that they are guaranteed a reward. This will stifle creativity and reduce their willingness to take risks or engage in challenging tasks in the future!

◆ **Quality of Learning:** Rewards could encourage memorization or rote learning, as children might focus more on completing a task to obtain a reward rather than on understanding or mastering a subject. This can affect the depth of learning and reduce the development of critical thinking skills! Can you remember what was on your 10th grade physics test? Probably not. You memorized info for a test, and it wasn't actually learned.

◆ **Social Relationships and Cooperation:** Reward systems can create competition rather than cooperation among children. This can lead to conflicts or a lack of collaborative skills, as children may focus on outperforming peers to gain rewards instead of working together and supporting each other's learning journeys.

◆ **Equity Issues:** Children's self-esteem can be affected negatively by extrinsic rewards if they see their classmates getting rewards that they don't have the capacity to receive based on the expectation!

In the end, are rewards more effective for the teacher or for the children? It can be effective as a band-aid solution for a hot second, but once intrinsic motivation is gone it is hard to come back from that. We have to support intrinsic motivation for kiddos. Play is the best way to allow children to explore their own interests on their own time and feel the value of their exploration—*intrinsically.*

Punishments

When behavior charts are used in classrooms to publicly display if a child is "good" or "bad," it can have severe consequences to not only the children but also the classroom environment and community as a whole. Here are a few reasons why behavior charts should never be used with children.

◆ **Stigmatization and Labeling:** As I just stated, behavior charts can unintentionally label children as "good" or "bad" based on their behavior (behavior itself is subjective and labeled based on an adult's mood at the time). This labeling can affect a child's self-esteem and self-concept, especially if they frequently find themselves on the "bad" end of the chart. Children may also stop playing with children who are always "on red" because they view that child as naughty.

◆ **Public Shaming:** Since behavior charts are often public, they can lead to shaming and embarrassment for those who are frequently on red or "clipped down." Can you imagine how embarrassing this can be? Children will not want to participate in other classroom activities for fear of further humiliation! My son was made to write his initials on the board for talking out of turn. I didn't know they did that anymore!

◆ **Reduced Intrinsic Motivation:** Just like extrinsic rewards, negative reinforcement like behavior charts can diminish intrinsic motivation in kids! When children are motivated to behave according to adults' expectations solely to avoid negative consequences or to advance on a behavior chart, they might not internalize or understand the genuine reasons for appropriate behavior, such as respecting others.

◆ **Focus on Compliance Rather Than Learning:** Behavior charts can shift the focus from learning and growth to mere compliance with rules. When children are focused on not getting clipped down, or performing in a way to get moved up, they aren't focused on being curious and the learning that happens through play.

◆ **Impaired Relationships:** Behavior charts don't build healthy relationships between teachers/caregivers and children. A child may not trust a teacher if they are constantly measuring their behavior on a chart on the wall that leaves them feeling defeated over and over. It can negatively impact relationships with other children, as I stated before, when someone won't play with someone else because they are "on red" a lot; it can also create extremely unhealthy power dynamics between the enforcer and the student. Think Miss Trunchbull from Matilda!

◆ **Ignoring the Root of the Behavior:** Behavior charts can oversimplify children's behaviors by not addressing the underlying causes. Children show us what their needs are through behaviors. Often, negative behaviors are because a child has unmet needs, they may be seeking a connection, or they may just be trying to learn about the world through trial and error!

◆ **Inequity and Bias:** Behavior management systems like charts can also reflect or draw attention to a teacher's biases. Decisions about what is "good" or "bad" behavior is subjective and influenced by the teacher's conscious or unconscious biases (and many times their mood that day), which can unfairly target certain students based on their background, personality, or other factors!

BUT Kristen, these are kids, and the behavior charts are in all of the school supply websites and everywhere on Pinterest. If so many people use them, then surely it's ok?

If you wouldn't impose a behavior chart, punishment, or reward on your coworkers, your employees, your spouse, or your friend, you shouldn't be doing it to children. You are not getting to the root of the issue with behavior charts. You are manipulating children to behave in a way that YOU think they should be behaving and these expectations are generally not developmentally appropriate.

BUT Kristen, how do I get kids to clean up after a massive paint explosion? What if they refuse?

Clean-up time is not the most developmentally appropriate time in an early childhood classroom. I am an adult, and I still don't like to clean up. To expect children to help clean up every mess they make isn't a developmentally appropriate expectation. This is a place where your adult ego may need to be left outside the classroom door and just recognize that a lot of the clean-up will fall on the shoulders of the adults in the room.

To get children to grow up to become adults who pitch in and help someone clean up, or clean up after themselves, they need to see adults modeling it every day. That is how they will learn how to get along in a community or group of people sharing the same materials.

If a child refuses to help, there could be many different things happening. Maybe it is overwhelming to them. Maybe they decided they didn't like the feeling of the paint on their fingers while they were painting and don't want to touch it again. Maybe they are on the brink of dysregulation and need to regulate. It is hard to pinpoint exactly why a child refuses to clean up. I let children refuse. Chances are they won't refuse forever if they see others modeling cleaning up. Let the child take a break under the table or hide in the corner of the classroom! They will come around eventually—even if it is to pick up one scrap of paper!

BUT Kristen, how do I deal with a student who hits and bites other kids? I've tried everything!

I am not a behavior expert and sometimes get baffled as well with certain behaviors that won't stop. Here is what I do know: When children can make choices about how they spend their time, who they spend it with, and what they engage with, they are much happier and more regulated. When children are supported in an environment that is developmentally appropriate for the age and stage they are in, they are much more content. This means that in a play-based, child-led environment when children are given ample time to play freely, the behaviors the adults label as "negative" are much less than in a traditional classroom. That being said, we will always have children showing us their needs aren't being met or that they are dysregulated by their behaviors and it is up to us to dig deeper to find the underlying cause. Behavior charts or extrinsic punishments or rewards won't keep a child from hitting or biting others for long. It is a short-term band-aid approach that is focused on what happens during and after the hitting or biting and not what is underlying or happens prior to the behavior.

References

Kohn, A. (2010). *Punished by Rewards: The Trouble with Gold Stars, Incentive Plans, A's, Praise, and Other Bribes*. Houghton Mifflin.

Manley, Travis. (2015) "Rip Those Behavior Charts off of the Wall and Burn Them." *Progressive Preceptors*. https://www.progressivepreceptors.com/blog/rip-those-behavior-charts-off-of-the-wall-and-burn-them

Maslow, A. H. (1943). A theory of human motivation. *Psychological Review*, *50*(4), 370–396.

Pica, R. (2021). *What If We Taught the Way Children Learn*. Corwin Press.

Ulber, J., Hamann, K., & Tomasello, M. (2016). Extrinsic Rewards Diminish Costly Sharing in 3-Year-Olds. *Child Development*, *87*(4), 1192–1203. https://doi.org/10.1111/cdev.12534

Zhang, Y., & Zheng, M. (2021). Noddings' Caring Education Theory and Its Enlightenment to School Education. *Frontiers in Educational Research*, *4*(6), 74–79. https://doi.org/10.25236/FER.2021.040614

13

Mermaids in the Woods

Rethinking recess and seeing the great outdoors as an extension of the classroom.

One day, out at forest school, deep in the woods, we came across a giant hole in the ground. It was rectangular-shaped, with rocks serving as a foundation to retain the earth. It was about six feet by eight feet and had been there a VERY long time. We eventually learned the hole was the foundation of an old farmhouse from the late 1800s. The children named it "The Hole," and that name still lives on to this day, being passed down from group to group each year!

To enter The Hole, which is approximately five-and-a-half feet deep, one must either jump in when there is snow or climb down using logs propped against the wall as a makeshift ladder for children to ascend and descend. The bottom of The Hole is covered in leaves and rocks and the children found some very old kettles and broken pieces of pottery buried in the compacted earth under their feet. The Hole serves as a foundation for a lot of lore and a lot of risk taking.

One day, it was a bit drizzly and gloomy, and I felt the children could use a little magic to bring us out of our funk. The other forest school teacher ran ahead during our hike into

DOI: 10.4324/9781003476719-14

the woods to plant seashells and colored gems in the bottom of the hole under the leaves for the children to find while they were playing.

On the hike in I told them a story about three mermaids that used to live in The Hole. It sounded something like this:

> I was reading something online about these woods and The Hole and it was SO interesting. Did you know that there used to be three mermaid sisters that lived here a long time ago? They spent most of their time in their pool, which happens to be The Hole where we play! It was like a bedroom for them, where they rested and stored treasures they didn't want anyone else to find. The coolest thing I learned was that they used the well as a slip-and-slide to get to the pond down the hill. They could quickly get to and from The Hole when there was danger or when it was time to relax and go to sleep at night. Isn't that so cool?

Of course the children had a million questions about the three mermaid sisters on the hike and I answered based on my completely made-up expertise on the topic.

When we got to The Hole, a group of children climbed in. It took a few minutes for them to discover their first treasure that had been planted by the teacher moments earlier. The children were in awe! "We found a seashell! I wonder if this was from the mermaids?" "I found a gem! This is the mermaids' treasures they were hiding!" The imaginations ran wild that morning and the mermaid play was on point. We found The Well nearby The Hole and the children imagined what the slip-and-slide looked like all the way down to the pond. The children asked if we could walk down by the pond to see if we could find any mermaids. So, of course we did! On the walk the children noticed that it had started to drizzle a bit of rain. They weren't bothered! We were prepared in our rain boots and rain suits. They wondered if the rain made the mermaids stay under water and if they ever played in the rain like we do. One child said, "I wonder if the mermaids like it sunny or rainy more?" The conversation then turned to children chatting about what type of weather they like the best.

And this is how children should learn about the weather. Being outdoors IN the weather. Having conversations that start organically because they are naturally noticing the weather and how their play changes based on the weather. Pondering and questioning based on what they experience.

The best place to learn about the weather is IN the weather. When it is safe, obviously. At Butterfly Hill, the children play outdoors in all weather conditions, including rainy, windy, snowy, and sunny for many hours each day. By getting to experience the weather and how it alters the outdoor classroom throughout the year, the children are able to categorize the concrete information they witness. This replaces the abstract concepts that children are presented with when singing songs about the weather and doing the weather on a chart. Remember, young children need concrete experiences!

Not only do children need to experience the weather to understand the weather, outdoor play is a necessity for young children. And it is disappearing from children's lives.

I read Richard Louv's book, *Last Child in the Woods* (2005) in 2012 and it changed my life. I had three little ones at the time and we were stressed out with ALLLLL the organized activities that I had to cart everyone to. Piano lessons, gymnastics, Tae Kwon Do, Girl Scouts, dance class.

Reading Louv's book made me sit back and think about my childhood and the wonderful memories I made running around our old farmhouse in Missouri with my sisters. We had a treehouse that felt like it was 25 feet in the air (I am sure it was probably about eight feet) that we had to use a rope ladder to get into. We would eat Bazooka bubblegum and look at our Garbage Pail Kids cards while the wind rustled the leaves around us. We would walk through the brambles and weeds to the old, dilapidated barn on our property, dodging venomous snakes and piles of coyote scat. At the barn we would walk through the pens that used to house pigs and we figured out how to stack old straw bales into a tower tall enough to climb into the hayloft. Once in the hayloft, we found an old rope swing hanging from the ceiling and tested it to make sure the whole roof wouldn't cave in if we put our weight on the swing. We would play outdoors all day until our mom hollered out the door to come have a meal. It was a magical time filled with memories that I will hold forever.

I realized that I was stealing precious outdoor time from my children by putting them in all of these organized activities. And I started to think: What if we had a place in our community that would facilitate children being outdoors when their adults at home can't? What if we re-imagined child care and preschool to look at our outdoor space as an extension of the indoor learning space, instead of a break from learning altogether? I started googling and learned about the concept of Nature Preschools and Forest Schools. It was at that moment that all of the information and knowledge I had been gathering over the years hit. I knew our community (and my own children) needed a place where they could be outdoors when their parents/guardians were at work. The idea of Butterfly Hill was born. I wanted children to get dirty enough that they'd leave a ring around the bathtub. I wanted children to have memories of treehouses, running around outdoors with friends, finding animal scat, and being able to learn through play in an environment that was safe and with teachers·who recognize the importance of outdoor play in childhood!

I came across a Persil Laundry Detergent "Free the Kids" ad campaign a few years ago, and it really shifted my perspective. The ad was filmed at Wabash Maximum Security Prison in Indiana, United States, and featured interviews with incarcerated individuals about their daily two-hour outdoor time. One man expressed how vital it was to him, saying, "[When I] have time to walk out that door and feel the sun on my face, that's everything to me." They described this outdoor time as crucial for maintaining mental well-being and physical strength.

The interviewer then asked how they would feel if their outdoor time was halved. The response was stark—devastating and torturous. A guard highlighted the potential disaster of reducing outdoor time to just an hour a day. When the interviewer pointed out that children often have only one hour of outdoor time daily, the men were taken aback, responding with comments like, "Wow," "That's depressing," and "I don't even know what to say to that." The ad ended with a poignant message: "On average, children spend less time outdoors than a prison inmate," accompanied by the imagery of prison doors closing (Dirt is Good, 2016).

It is essential that we get children outdoors. When I was teaching in the traditional preschool classroom, we only got outdoors if we had gotten through all of the indoor things first. To top it off, if the slides were wet from sprinkles or morning dew, we didn't go outdoors. I just accepted this as "this is the way it's always been done" so I never really questioned it until I read Louv's book and started really reflecting on my teaching practice as it relates to outdoor play and learning. There are many reasons why children don't get outdoors in early childhood and, in this case, it was because it was inconvenient for the teachers.

Getting kids outdoors isn't just about fun; it's a brain boost! Studies show that being in nature helps their brains grow. When teachers are advocates for getting kids outside, they're helping children build super-smart brains!

> The "richness and novelty" of being outdoors stimulates brain development (Rivkin 2000). Research shows that "direct, ongoing experience of nature in relatively familiar settings remains a vital source for children's physical, emotional, and intellectual development" (Kellert 2004). Proximity to, views of, and daily exposure to natural settings increases children's ability to focus and enhances cognitive abilities (Wells, 2000).
>
> (Cooper, 2015)

So what are some of the reasons we keep children indoors?

◆ **Technology and Screens:** There is a popular statistic which says that, on average, children spend four to seven minutes outdoors per day and five to eight hours behind a screen. That is shocking. And unacceptable. If parents or caregivers struggle to get children outdoors during the limited time they have with them each evening, it's

ESSENTIAL that we get them outdoors during their time with us.

◆ **Organized/Structured Activities:** Children are in sports and other adult-directed activities outside of child care/ preschool hours. If THEY aren't in sports, chances are they're being carted to and fro as their older siblings participate in organized activities. And even if these activities take place outdoors, they don't gain the benefits of free play in outdoor spaces. "In general, inviting play and providing physical indoor and outdoor environments that support a variety of play types in ECEC affords children opportunities to gain essential bodily, social, and cultural experiences. As shown in this study, play is strongly related to children's well-being and involvement, and will as such be important to provide good psychosocial- and learning environments" (Storli & Sandseter, 2019).

◆ **Lack of Accessible Green Spaces:** As urban areas expand and become more densely populated, access to safe and inviting green spaces is lacking for families and schools in these areas. Children living in cities might not have easy access to parks, yards, or other outdoor areas!

◆ **Safety Concerns:** Parents/guardians are concerned about their children's safety. This includes fears about traffic, the risk of a child getting hurt, and the possibility of encountering strangers. These concerns can lead parents to keep children indoors where they feel it is safer.

◆ **Changes in Family Dynamics:** With more households having two working parents or single-parent families, there might be less time for supervising children outdoors. Two working parents means children are in child care/ preschool, so it is OUR duty to ensure they get outdoors!

Despite the multitude of reasons for keeping kids indoors, outdoor play in natural environments has a positive impact on children's overall health and development. Green spaces like parks and gardens reduce stress, aggression, and mental fatigue, promoting better focus and emotional well-being. Additionally, playing outside enhances physical fitness, coordination, balance, and agility, encouraging higher levels of physical activity among children.

> Time spent in green spaces, including parks, play areas, and gardens, has been shown to reduce stress and mental fatigue (Taylor 2001). In one study children who were exposed to greener environments in a public housing area demonstrated less aggression and violence and less mental stress (Kuo & Sullivan 2001). Just viewing nature reduces physiological stress response, increases level of interest and attention, and decreases feelings of fear and anger or aggression (Burdette & Whitaker 2005). […] Children who play outdoors are generally more fit than those who spend the majority of their time inside. Children who play outside in natural areas also show a statistically significant improvement in motor fitness with better coordination, balance, and agility (Fjortoft 2001). The mere presence (with no additional programming) of an outdoor learning environment with natural features and a looping pathway is associated with a 22% increase in physical activity (Cosco, Moore, Smith, 2014). Children's physical activity is motivated by diverse outdoor environments (Boldemann et al, 2006) and the preschool outdoors is a determinant of preschool physical activity (Cardon et al 2008).
>
> (Cooper, 2015)

What if we stopped looking at outdoor time as recess, and instead considered it an extension of the indoor learning environment? I love to preach that almost anything that can be done *indoors*, can be done *outdoors* as well. It just takes adults who are willing to get past their own inconveniences to make it happen! Sure, it CAN be more work to take play outdoors and provide yet another rich learning environment outside. But nature actually provides a lot of it. Here are some things that you can do to make your outdoor playspace more engaging and wondrous for the children:

◆ Add loose parts! Grab some plastic totes and fill them with things like old coffee containers, ice cream buckets, branch blocks, pinecones, traffic cones, balls, scrap wood (slivers sanded down!), car tires, PVC pipe, old rain gutters, balls, wheelbarrows, shovels, ice cube trays, stumps, logs, rocks etc.

◆ Bring art materials outdoors! Have a caddy ready to go with popular art supplies. Use clipboards to keep the children's papers from flying away.

◆ Have circle time outdoors! Who said you have to do it inside? You can also eat snacks outdoors, lunch, or even let them rest outside!

◆ Bring traditional play items outdoors: Plastic baby dolls, dress up clothes, books, and musical instruments are often only reserved for indoors, but why not bring them out?

On the topic of loose parts, there is large amounts of evidence that shows how important they are for the early childhood environment. (Check out Chapter 14!)

> The type and quality of play can be significantly influenced by the physical environment of a playspace …. Outdoor environments tend to offer a more enriched environment for play, affording more varied and less structured play opportunities, which in turn can stimulate creativity, facilitate learning and support physical development …. Outdoors spaces which provide opportunities for engagement with nature and natural materials have been shown to foster more varied and complex play, as well as positively contribute to children's physical, emotional and social development …. Environments which provide more diverse play affordances can also engage a broader spectrum of children and for longer periods of time.
>
> (Loebach & Cox, 2022)

BUT Kristen, you mentioned letting children play with sticks outdoors, how do you handle that so no one gets an eye poked out?

One year, during our annual first aid training, I asked the EMT (emergency medical technician) teaching the class how many times she has ever seen a child get poked in the eye with a stick in her 20 years working as an EMT. She said never.

The dreaded stick play. In my traditional years, we wouldn't even let children pick them up. The stick is the world's oldest loose part and toy! It is the magic wand of childhood! It is the gun that will shoot the deer for dinner. It is the pencil to draw one's name in the mud. A stick can be anything! Keeping children from imaginative stick play is taking away a huge part of childhood. The stick was actually nominated into The Strong National Museum of Play in 2008. We need to allow children to use this amazing tool/toy/loose part while they are in our care.

Here are a few things teachers can do to help ease their fears around stick play in early childhood environments:

♦ **Supervise:** Always supervise children when they are playing with sticks, especially younger children who may not fully understand potential risks and may not have the body awareness or self-regulation to keep their sticks away from the bodies of other children.

♦ **Teach Safe Handling:** Teach children how to handle sticks safely, emphasizing that they should never run or play rough while holding a stick. Show them how to hold the stick away from their bodies and others. We encourage children to drag sticks behind them on the ground when they are transporting them from one area to another!

♦ **Select Appropriate Sticks:** Encourage the children to choose sticks that are sturdy and free from sharp, splintered edges. Avoid sticks that are taller than a child's body, have many offshoot branches, or have pointed ends. Or, ensure that your playspace only has sticks that are teacher approved before they even head outside for the day!

♦ **Establish Boundaries:** A teacher could set boundaries for stick play. Give children a designated YES area where they CAN play with sticks. Ensure they understand not to swing sticks near other children.

♦ **Encourage Creativity:** Encourage children to use sticks for things like building forts or creating nature art.

♦ **Communicate with Other Teachers and Parents/ Guardians:** If stick play is a YES, ensure that all other teachers know the boundaries and limits so children are given the same opportunities to play no matter which adult is facilitating play. It is also a good idea to make sure parents know the benefits of stick play and that you have done risk assessments to ensure the children are safe!

BUT Kristen, the kids could get hurt if we let them take risks outdoors…

"Recent estimates show that children would need to spend about three hours per day playing, every day, for 10 years before they were likely to get an injury that needed treatment (and it would likely still be minor)" (CBC, 2021). In my eight years as the founding director of Butterfly Hill, we had one child get a stitch in their forehead. This could have happened to her walking outside of her home or in front of Target.

Children need risk taking! If we don't allow children to take risks, it would be like never letting a child hold a pencil for their development!

> Risky Play has multiple benefits for the physical, cognitive, and social development of young children. Risk-taking in play helps children test their physical limits, develop their perceptual-motor capacity, and learn to avoid and adjust to dangerous environments and activities (Brussoni et al., 2012).
>
> (Liu & Birkeland, 2022)

There are many types of risks but I am specifically referencing physical risk here. Risk isn't just climbing trees and jumping off of tall things. Risk can be walking on a fallen log with no shoes on. Risk can be swinging on a swing they have never tried before.

Many times when an early childhood teacher thinks about risk, they immediately jump to hazard. They are different. A hazard is a child balancing on a fallen tree that has a ton of broken branches underneath it without a teacher nearby to guide them and help if needed. A teacher can help children take risks by applying some forethought to the space. If there is a place that children are naturally drawn to climb, a teacher could put mulch down under that space as a fall zone.

Resilience is a treasured trait in both adults and children. However, teaching resilience requires exposing children to healthy risks. They must learn to assess risks independently and make suitable decisions. Providing a risk-friendly environment is crucial for them to practice and develop this skill.

BUT Kristen, not everyone comes with the proper outdoor clothing.

◆ Ask for gently used apparel donations from the community! People are SO willing to help with clothing/ gear donations when they know they are going to a good cause! Over time you will get quite a collection.

◆ Ask for donations when the children in the classroom outgrow their gear and when they leave your program for grade school! You can get quite a collection that way!

◆ If you have a stockpile of extra outdoor gear on hand, you can outfit the kiddos who don't come prepared.

◆ It is also imperative that you have a guide for parents/ guardians that describes what types of gear their child needs to have each day when they come. If they know this up front, chances are they will be more agreeable and able to find outdoor gear for their child.

◆ In the community where I live, there are programs that give outdoor clothing away for free to families that can't afford to purchase outdoor clothing. Connect with organizations like those for the families in your care!

BUT Kristen, if they get dirty, the parents/guardians will get upset.
Our motto at Butterfly Hill was "If you didn't get dirty, you didn't play." Our work shirts said this on the back, and we had a plaque by the door leading out to the parking lot for parents to see every day that said the same thing! If the parents/guardians know up front that outdoor play is essential and a part of their child's day, they will know that their child may come home dirty.

Some cultures and communities associate dirt with uncleanliness and therefore don't want their children to look dirty. If this is the case, have baby wipes or other cleaning cloths on hand to clean up the kiddos before they leave. Have each child keep a change of clothes at school so they can change before they head home for the day.

BUT Kristen, we have to share the playground with other classes.

A good friend of mine used to teach preschool in a public school and had to share the playground with all the other grades. They did have a tiny little outdoor space that was fenced in full of loose parts and dirt for digging. To get children outdoors more, they would walk across the school parking lot and field to get to a low-land, ditch area that was overgrown with brush. The children made that area their own and preferred to play here rather than on the commercial school playground. Time stood still as the children weaved the willows into braids, hung ribbons from branches, and wore a slide into the slope of the ditch. This "enchanted forest" was a rare place and fully forgotten by the adults. The children see magic in any outdoor space, whether it is a playground or an overgrown ditch!

Get creative. Is there a nearby area where children can explore and play outdoors, extending beyond the typical playground setting? Only have access to a rooftop playspace? Go up there in the morning when no one else is there and have storytime and music and movement up there!

References

CBC. (2021, June 29). Risky Play for Children: Why We Should Let Kids Go Outside and Then Get Out. CBC's Nature of Things. https://www.cbc.ca/natureofthings/features/risky-play-for-children-why-we-should-let-kids-go-outside-and-then-get-out

Cooper, A. (2015). Nature and the Outdoor Learning Environment: The Forgotten Resource in Early Childhood Education. *International Journal of Early Childhood Environmental Education, 3*(1).

Dirt is Good. (2016, March 21). Free the Kids [Video file]. Retrieved from https://youtu.be/8Q2WnCkBTw0?si=HkH524jMkpnkJ9FC

Liu, J., & Birkeland, A. (2022) Perceptions of Risky Play Among Kindergarten Teachers in Norway and China. *International Journal of Early Childhood, 54*(3), 339–360.

Loebach, J., & Cox, A. (2022). Playing in "The Backyard': Environmental Features and Conditions of a Natural Playspace Which Support Diverse Outdoor Play Activities among Younger Children. *International Journal of Environmental Research and Public Health*, *19*(19), 12661.

Louv, R. (2005). *Last Child in the Woods: Saving Our Children from Nature-Deficit Disorder*. Algonquin Books.

Storli, R., & Sandseter, E. B. H. (2019). Children's Play, Well-Being and Involvement: How Children Play Indoors and Outdoors in Norwegian Early Childhood Education and Care Institutions. *International Journal of Play*, *8*(1), 65–78. https://doi.org/10.1080/21594937.2019.1580338

14

A Room Full of Junk

Loose parts are teachers themselves!

When I was teaching in the classroom at Butterfly Hill, I loved to take all of the plastic play food out of the kitchen and replace it with random items; things like leather and fabric scraps, rubber bands, napkin rings, tealight candles, stacks of cups, and colored wood blocks. After a bit of confusion from the children, they would settle in to use their new "food" to create meals for their friends and teachers. One child made an elaborate tablescape that would rival the best Instagram-worthy charcuterie board. Using wooden napkin rings, leather wall painting sponges, tea light candles, coasters that were crocheted, a tiered dessert tray, and a spinning lazy susan in the center, Lo created the most inviting meal for her classmates and babydoll! She didn't see napkin rings; they were donuts. She didn't see coasters; she saw pancakes. She didn't see leather wall-painting sponges; she saw cheeseburgers!

The items that were placed into the children's play kitchen are known as "loose parts" in the early childhood industry. Loose parts are those wonderful, versatile materials that are often found in recycling bins. They're open-ended and movable, allowing children to let their imaginations run wild and turn these items into anything they can dream up.

DOI: 10.4324/9781003476719-15

If you've ever taught in an early childhood classroom, chances are you've had loose parts in some form, even if you didn't realize it. The original loose part? Wood blocks. A wood block can be a cell phone, a boat, a brick in a building, or a slice of banana bread! Loose parts take the concept of wood blocks and elevates it!

The term "loose parts" was coined by architect Simon Nicholson in the 1970s. Nicholson introduced the concept of loose parts in his article titled "How Not to Treat Children: The Child in the City," published in Landscape Architecture magazine in 1971. He proposed that loose parts, which he defined as materials that can be moved, combined, redesigned, and taken apart and put back together in multiple ways, are essential for fostering creativity, imagination, and exploration in children's play environments.

A toy car will only ever be a toy car. There isn't a lot of imagination a child can exercise other than where the car is going or how it is moving. A castle will likely stay a castle. A plastic horse will likely live its toy life as a horse. A princess dress will always be a princess dress. Compare that with loose parts. Loose parts are open ended, so they can be anything! Fabric scarves can be a princess dress AND a cheetah costume. Large wood blocks can be a castle AND an oven. A stick can be a horse AND a magic wand. Loose parts are one of the best non-inventions of all time to get children curious and spark creativity!

We can take loose parts theory all the way back to Jean Piaget. Though he didn't use the term loose parts, Piaget's developmental theory relates to loose parts play through its emphasis on the importance of play in cognitive development and the construction of knowledge. Piaget proposed that children actively construct their understanding of the world through interactions with their environment. To me, this closely aligns with the open-ended exploration and experimentation and imagination that is encouraged through loose parts play.

Loose parts play provides children with a variety of materials and objects that can be manipulated, combined, and transformed, according to children's imagination and creativity. This type of play allows children to engage in hands-on exploration, problem-solving, and symbolic representation, which are key to Piaget's theory of cognitive development (Piaget, 1952).

One of my favorite memories was walking into the classroom and seeing a child laying flat on his belly, airplane style, on top of a big wooden truck. He had a toilet plunger (new and meant for play) in each hand. He swung his arms forward, suctioning the plungers to the floor ahead of him, then used the suction as momentum to pull himself and the truck forward. He then worked to unstick the plungers from the floor and swung his arms forward to repeat over and over as he propelled his new machine forward! So genius!

In a world where kids hear so many NOs, isn't it refreshing for them to be able to play with open-ended toys in whatever way they see fit? Can I use these sticks to design an ant shelter? YES! Could I take this cloth and build a mini hammock? Yes! Can I create a funny mustache contest using sticky notes and a marker? Yes, yes, yes!

One very cold winter, the teachers at Butterfly Hill and I decided to replace many of the toys and loose parts in the classroom with all different sized cardboard boxes and colored masking tape. The creativity that emerged was awe inspiring to watch. Children spent hours using their imagination and problem-solving skills to cut, tape, paint, marker, move, and stack the cardboard boxes to make a world of their own in the classroom. There were traps, baby doll beds, animal cages, dollhouses, shields and swords, caves, trains, airplanes, and rocketships.

I watched three little ones stack milk crates on top of a wooden pallet to create a ship when they were in the outdoor classroom. They were sailing to South Dakota! They used composite decking samples (a great loose part for outdoors that never rots!) as their GPS to navigate, and were blurting out numbers and codes (their coordinates) of where they were heading. The wind started to pick up and this led to them shifting their play, and their ship started to sink! They created a ship mast from a piece of PVC pipe and some paper and used a large stick as their oar. The wind continued to strengthen, which led them to shift their play again: their ship started to sink! It turns out that one of the children was very interested in the Titanic and was bringing their prior knowledge and interests into the play. The teamwork, problem-solving, rich language, and child-led learning were on point that morning!

Aside from the occasional donation or garage sale find of traditional-looking toys, the environment at Butterfly Hill is carefully designed to get children curious, to get them designing, to get them creating, and to get them questioning. Filled with items that may look like junk to the untrained eye, the shelves are stocked with materials that allow children the autonomy to use their imagination and spark their creative thinking.

Once I started shifting away from the preprogrammed toy mindset to one of purposefully selecting materials that were open ended, I saw the creativity soar in my preschool classroom. I was able to shake off my adult goggles and what I thought materials should be used for and allow the children to use their own imaginations and ideas to use materials in all new ways. Children are SO creative if the stodgy adults step back and let them use their own ideas!

I am not saying that traditional toys should be removed completely from your spaces. There is nothing wrong with having a basket of farm animals, cars, or baby dolls. There is a place for those items and we had them on the shelves at Butterfly Hill. I am suggesting to add in some open-ended materials and let the children get creative!

Kim Atkinson, at the University of Victoria, suggests that many of the toys in classrooms and the ways that educators use them are simply automatic assumptions rather than purposeful pedagogical decisions.

> While I am not suggesting that toys are bad and should be removed from early years settings, I would argue that critical reflection on materials and environments might open possibilities for seeing and thinking differently. The many unseen assumptions embedded in materials and environments limit who children and teachers can be. Recognizing the social, cultural, commercial, and scientific discourses through which the "truths" of early learning materials have emerged allows for new questions and new conversations

to begin. If we are to embrace an image of the child as competent, capable constructors of theories, and an image of teachers as co-researchers alongside children, then we must also reconsider materials and environments.

(Atkinson, 2015)

Here is a short list of some of my favorite loose parts to have on hand:

- Silicone baking cups
- Sponges of all shapes and textures
- Containers of all sizes
- Lids from anything (applesauce, baby food, milk cartons, pickle jars)
- Paper towel tubes
- Egg cartons
- Wine corks
- Napkin rings
- Fabric scarves
- Clothespins
- Sticky notes
- Duplo® blocks
- Magna-tiles®
- Wood planks
- Sticks/twigs
- Rocks
- House gutter pieces
- Balls of all sizes and textures
- Pinecones
- Ribbon/yarn
- Sheer curtain panels
- Cardboard

If we are in the business of providing an environment that promotes developmentally appropriate practice, loose parts are one of the ways that we can support children. By observing children engaging in loose parts play, we can tailor our teaching methods, curriculum, and interactions to match the developmental stage, needs, and interests of each child in our care. We can create supportive learning environments that foster social, emotional, cognitive, and physical growth while recognizing the uniqueness of each child!

In a time when technology is moving so fast, we need to raise up humans that can think fast, evolve along with the world, and think divergently. When children are given access to open-ended materials like boxes, sand, sticks, Magna-tiles®, they are able to exercise their creativity and divergent thinking!

In an article titled "The Dead Tree: Reconsidering Toys in Early Years Spaces," published by the journal *Canadian Children*, author Kim Atkinson writes about a time when children played with a dead tree in the preschool yard:

> The children who played with the dead tree in the preschool yard created stories and imagined possible worlds. The tree itself carried stories, perhaps of forests and holidays, but it did not prescribe particular uses or ways of being. A dead tree carries no expectations, no history of how it should be played with or understood. There is no wrong way to use a dead tree. There are no boundaries limiting character roles, dialogues, and scripts.
>
> (Atkinson, 2015)

Extracting the learning from loose parts play (like in the story of the dead tree) requires a teacher to observe and reflect on the play that is taking place. Through careful observation of play, educators can offer children objects and materials that develop their sense of wonder and engagement (Curtis et al., 2013).

> When we offer meaningful materials to children and study the details of their actions to identify the significance they hold, we become intellectually engaged with children in their pursuits. We understand the role we play in providing vital materials and opportunities to explore and learn.
>
> (Curtis et al., 2013)

When we provide children with loose parts and allow them the freedom to create as they wish, we're not just offering them materials; we're opening a window into their thoughts and experiences. This form of play gives us a unique glimpse into their cognitive and emotional worlds. We can observe the stories they are processing, whether it's through building a castle, playing cheetah with friends, or reenacting scenes from their favorite cartoons or even their lives! These creations often reflect the narratives they're grappling with, the challenges they're trying to understand, and the joys they wish to express.

Loose parts play also unveils children's values and curiosities! And we know that curiosity is the spark that ignites the learning that happens in childhood! The objects they choose, the ways they combine them, and the stories they tell reveal what matters to them. It could be a fascination with nature, a love for storytelling, an interest in construction and engineering, or a desire to explore fantastical realms. By observing these creations, educators gain insights into students' interests, passions, and areas of strength for each child in their care!

Reflecting on and harnessing these insights is where the real magic happens! Educators can use these nuggets of understanding to tailor learning experiences that resonate deeply with students. For instance, if a child frequently builds structures related to animals, this could spark projects or discussions about habitats, ecosystems, or animal behaviors. If a student consistently incorporates storytelling elements, a teacher could create a puppet theater to encourage more storytelling!

In the end, teachers can use the observations from loose parts play to create a learning environment that remains relevant, engaging, and fresh. This approach not only fosters meaningful learning experiences but also encourages a sense of connection, community, and empowerment as students see their interests and ideas valued and integrated into the classroom.

BUT Kristen, I have never introduced loose parts into my classroom, how do I do it? Do I teach the children how to use the materials?

Well, let's think about wood blocks. When the children started on day 1, did you explicitly teach how to engage and play with the wood blocks? I am assuming not. You more than likely allowed children to take them off the shelves and use them in any way they wanted! This is exactly how you do it with all other loose parts! Just put them on the shelf, floor, or table and let the children's ideas take over. It is when we insert our own adult ideas that children's creativity is stifled.

My advice is to start small. Start with one basket of loose part material. Put it on the shelf or table and let children take over! After a few days, add another basket of something else in the same area. Continue to add or subtract based on children's engagement and your own comfort level!

BUT Kristen, we have a tight budget and I can't go out and purchase more things!

That's the cool thing about loose parts; generally, you can get pretty creative and use things that you would recycle. I have found amazing loose parts on the side of the road! One that comes to mind is a giant pink crystal-looking curtain rod finial—the children went gaga over that piece! Items like box packing paper, container lids, game pieces, egg cartons, paper towel tubes, wine corks, used party decorations, and clean yogurt or baby food containers are free and can be used in any area of the classroom environment!

Ask the families for donations! Give them a list of recyclable items they can collect. You will build up an amazing collection very quickly just by doing this!

BUT Kristen, I have tried putting loose parts out and it becomes a huge mess! Some children just like to dump the baskets out and don't even play with any of it. Then I have to clean up the mess!

Have you ever heard of the Play Schema Theory? Good ol' Piaget is to be thanked again for his work around schema play as he recognized patterns in children's play and applied the word *schema* to children's repetitive behaviors (Piaget, 1952). Many other researchers and educators have added to the theory of play schema and more and more play schema are being identified all the time.

In her book, *Schemas, A Practical Handbook*, Laura England describes schema as "patterns of behaviour that allow young children to construct knowledge and understanding of how the world works" (England, 2018).

The dumping of loose parts is recognized as the filling and emptying play schema. Children enjoy filling containers, purses, baskets, with items and then dumping them out. My favorite was finding purses filled with random things at the end of the day!

We can shift our mindset to understand that even though it looks like a child is "just dumping," they are playing! The dumping *is* their learning and play. Even though it may drive adults bananas, the child is learning!

If you want to keep children from dumping loose parts from baskets, you need to ensure that you have ample opportunities for children to fill and dump in other areas of the classroom. If you notice particular children doing this repeatedly, they are letting you know that they are enjoying the filling and emptying play schema. You can redirect them to the sensory table filled with sand, scoops, containers, and funnels! Or, just let them continue to dump the loose parts… afterall the dumping *is* the play and it is therefore valid!

BUT Kristen, when I have introduced loose parts like sticks or PVC pipes in the past, they use them as weapons!

In my experience in the classroom, children who are trying to sort out the world around them will end up using ANY material as a weapon. They will use their fingers if they don't have a PVC pipe. They will use Duplo® blocks to build a gun. They will use a wood block as a grenade. Whatever their lived or learned experiences are, they will try to sort out things they don't understand through play. I don't blame loose parts on bringing in the weapon play; it may amplify it, but it is not the cause. We can't shield our children from their experiences outside the classroom, but we can choose to understand it and support children who are trying to figure out the world around them.

I do believe that it is responsible to acknowledge that many children grow up around violence. Either in their home, on TV and the news, in the neighborhood and even sometimes in their country at large. Many children aren't privileged to live in a community where playing with pretend weapons is safe (most notably, Black and Brown children). In these instances, it is OK to explain to children the reasons why weapon play isn't a safe way to play and to work with children to come up with different ways they can use their loose parts.

Because the program I founded is located in a relatively safe, middle-class, and predominantly White community, I thought it would be important to amplify the voice of a Black person who has lived experience growing up in community grappling with crime to ensure that these important voices are not erased. Here are important words about weapon play from Kisa Marx, a Black play practitioner (and dear friend) who believes childhood is sacred and play is revolutionary:

I wholeheartedly agree with Kristen's perspective on children using any material to fashion weapons. It seems to me that they engage in such play as they grapple with complex concepts like power, morality, and justice in a world where they often feel powerless. Growing up in a neighborhood rife with crime, my twin sister and I were bombarded with messages of violence. However, our imaginative play with pretend weapons never mirrored the crime we witnessed on the streets. We were always cowboys, never cops, and the notion of being gangbangers never even crossed our minds during playtime.

Our intention was never to replicate our harsh reality; rather, we sought to understand these concepts in a way that was far removed from our actual experiences. Despite it being strictly forbidden in our household, we persisted in our play until our ill understanding matured, at which point, those childhood games became distant memories. To me, weapon play is no different from any other form of imaginative play. Children immerse themselves in it as they repeatedly enact certain actions, just like they do in other forms of schematic play. Just as they wrap everything up to understand enveloping or covet every bag to grasp transportation, they continuously seek out and create weapons until they comprehend the complexities of good versus bad, power dynamics, and justice.

This is precisely why there should be room for dialogue, especially with children from communities like ours with heightened crime rates. Shaming, reprimanding, or harshly punishing children for engaging in weapon play doesn't mitigate the risks; rather, it exacerbates them. By silencing the child's natural curiosity, we deny them the opportunity to explore and understand the world around them. These profound questions are left to simmer without an outlet, and although playing with PVC pipes, Duplo blocks, or finger guns poses no real threat of violence, the child now knows that their curiosity isn't safe to express.

Shutting down these conversations only hinders a child's development and understanding. We must create environments where children feel safe to explore, question, and learn, even if it means engaging with uncomfortable topics.

BUT Kristen, I have infants and toddlers and lots if the traditional loose parts are choking hazards. Any ideas for loose parts for infants and toddlers?

Loose parts are essential for infants and toddlers. If you've ever had an older infant, you know they love to get into the kitchen cabinets and pull out all the bowls and containers! Let's expand on this and offer small children large containers, lids, silicone baking pans or candy molds, silicone cupcake liners, silicone sponges, kitchen utensils like large wooden or plastic spoons, ice cube trays, wool dryer balls, scarves or pieces of fabric, and measuring cups. All are washable if they put them in their mouth! When you start to use your own creativity, you will see loose parts EVERYWHERE! The options are endless when we see materials in a different way and imagine what they *could* be versus what they *are*.

Just because you might be limited in the size of loose parts (small parts = choking hazard), don't forget about textures! Cutting boards, cups, papers, milk cartons come in a variety of materials. Fabric scraps feel different when they're wet versus dry—or even frozen!

References

Atkinson, K. (2015). The Dead Tree: Reconsidering Toys in Early Years Spaces. *Canadian Children, 40*(3), 56–60.

Curtis, D., Brown, K. L., Baird, L., & Coughlin, A. M. (2013). Planning Environments and Materials That Respond to Young Children's Lively Minds. *YC: Young Children, 68*(4), 26–31.

England, L. (2018). *Schemas: A Practical Handbook*. Featherstone.

Nicholson, S. (1971). How Not to Treat Children: The Child in the City. *Landscape Architecture*, *62*(1), 30–33.

Piaget, J. (1952). *The Origins of Intelligence in Children* (M. Cook, Trans.). International Universities Press.

15

Sharing is NOT Caring

Sharing isn't caring; teaching children to take turns is.

A few years into my early childhood teaching career, I was starting to reflect on all the things that we do as adults that we don't allow children to do; the double standards that exist between being an adult and being a small child. The first big double standard that came up was *sharing*.

A girlfriend of mine came over to my house a few years ago to hang out and drink coffee. I started telling her about this really good novel I was reading and that she should read it. She said, "Sharing is caring," and demanded that I hand the book over because she wanted to read it right away. I responded, "I'm not done with it. I'll let you know when I'm finished, and then you may borrow it." That didn't sit well with her. "How about you can read it for five minutes and then I can read it for five minutes? We can set a timer."

OK, that didn't really happen, but can you see the double standard here? Most adults wouldn't readily give up the juicy novel they're engrossed in simply because someone else asked for a turn. You actually probably wouldn't want that person to be your friend anymore if they acted that way.

When I started out teaching, "Sharing is caring!" and "You need to share!" were both phrases that would come out of my mouth regularly. They were an automatic response when conflict

DOI: 10.4324/9781003476719-16

erupted in the classroom or with my own children when they were young. This was a concept I hadn't deeply explored, and my auto response kicked in whenever someone desired what another person had. Conflict made me uncomfortable, and I didn't have the tools at that point in my career to really reflect on the ramifications of forced sharing among children.

A few years into my early childhood teaching career, I starting to reflect on all the things that we do as adults that we don't allow children to do. When I put the concept of "Sharing is Caring" into an adult perspective, I understood how utterly nonsensical forced sharing is.

Forced sharing is not caring. Forcing a child to give up something they're actively engaged with takes away from their learning experience. It is giving them the message that someone else's needs and wants are more important than theirs. In her book *It's OK Not to Share* (2012), author Heather Shumaker emphasizes the important distinction between *encouraging* and *forcing* children to share. If sharing doesn't occur on the child's terms, they learn that sharing feels bad. It doesn't teach generosity; it actually stifles it because it's not done in an authentic way.

What I started to do was teach children to take turns. I taught them to use language similar to what I would use if someone asked me if they could read the novel I'm currently enjoying.

Here's language to teach children when learning to take turns:

- ◆ "I'm not done yet, but I will let you know when I am done so you can have a turn."
- ◆ "I am using it right now. You can have a turn when I am done."
- ◆ "You can use it when I am done."
- ◆ "Can I have a turn when you are done?"

Let's dig a little deeper into why young children might resist sharing, unveiling some of the underlying processes in their brains when they're asked to give up a toy they're playing with.

- ◆ **Egocentrism and Self-Centeredness:** Young children are egocentric. This means they generally see the world from their own perspective and have difficulty understanding the feelings and needs of others. Adults generally have a hard time when other adults are self-centered and egocentric. But don't worry; young children are still developing, and this more than likely subsides as they grow! Because dealing with egocentric behavior can be challenging for adults, it can be frustrating when children hoard toys or exhibit possessive behavior.

◆ **Concrete Operational Thinking:** I've got some Piaget theory here for you again. Piaget's theory of cognitive development explains that children in the preoperational stage (ages two to seven) often aren't ready for abstract thinking and are more focused on concrete, tangible aspects of their environment. This can lead to a possessiveness towards toys and other items, as they see them as immediate extensions of themselves.

◆ **Limited Impulse Control:** Now for some brain science stuff. Stay with me here. The prefrontal cortex, responsible for self-control and executive functions, is not fully developed in young children. This limited impulse control can contribute to behaviors that are impulsive, like grabbing a shovel from another child and not wanting to share. They act on their immediate wants without thinking through the consequences.

◆ **Attachment and Security:** A bit more theory for you. Attachment Theory lets us know that young children form strong emotional bonds with their primary caregivers. In unfamiliar situations, like the beginning of a new school year or when feeling insecure, children may look for comfort and familiarity through possessions and things, leading to hogging a toy all day long.

◆ **Social Learning:** Children learn by observing and imitating the behavior of others, especially adults, and maybe even siblings or other children in the classroom. If a child observes possessive behavior or a lack of turn taking modeled by adults or older siblings, they are more likely to imitate these behaviors.

♦ **Development of Empathy:** Empathy, the ability to understand and share the feelings of others, develops gradually (a more in depth look at this in a bit). Young children may not yet fully grasp the concept of how their actions impact others emotionally, making it hard for them to empathize and willingly give something up for the sake of someone else.

♦ **Sense of Autonomy:** Toddlers and preschoolers are often in the process of developing a sense of autonomy and independence. Possessing and controlling toys and other items can be a way for them to exercise their independence and establish a sense of ownership over something.

Now that we know brain science, theory, and developmental reasons behind why it can be challenging for children to share something they're engaged with, we realize that forcing them to share doesn't foster the skills we hope they'll learn from phrases like, "You need to share" or "Sharing is caring." A child will learn to share on their own terms and in their own time. It takes patience on the part of the adults in the room and an understanding of child development.

BUT Kristen, if we don't teach children to share, they won't develop empathy.

Forcing children to share or taking turns on a timer might achieve compliance among the children in the short term, but it doesn't necessarily promote the development of *true* empathy. Empathy is best nurtured when children have opportunities to understand and navigate their emotions in a supportive environment. Could we shift the narrative from "sharing is caring" to "taking turns is caring?"

Young children need the freedom to make choices and assert control over their belongings. Afterall, young children don't often have control or power in their lives. Forcing them to share can lead to frustration and may not help them understand the perspective of others. True empathy involves recognizing and understanding the feelings of others. Instead of forcing sharing, teachers can focus on helping children identify and express their own emotions and encouraging them to recognize emotions of others in the classroom.

Here are some things you can do to encourage the development of empathy in young children…

◆ Be a role model! Demonstrate empathetic behavior in your interactions with children and other adults in the room. Narrate your own emotions and express empathy towards others in the classroom. You can say things like, "I can see you're feeling sad because you wanted to play with that toy. How about we find something else you might enjoy?"

◆ Introduce books and stories that highlight characters experiencing various emotions. Discuss the characters' feelings with the children and ask open-ended questions to encourage children to share their thoughts and empathize with the characters.

◆ One of our largest roles in the classroom during free play is social and emotional coaching. Teach children problem-solving skills by guiding them through conflicts. Provide language around feelings. Encourage them to communicate with each other, express their feelings, and work together to find solutions! This aids in fostering a sense of empathy and cooperation among the children.

◆ Utilize meal and snack times to talk about children's experiences, feelings, and perspectives in small group and one-on-one conversation. This can build a sense of community and encourages children to listen and respond empathetically to their peers.

◆ Plan collaborative projects that require teamwork. This could involve building structures or creating artwork that everyone can add to. How about having a big piece of cardboard on the easel with various mark-making materials that any child can add to over a few days?

We CAN create an environment that prioritizes emotional understanding, communication, and collaboration without forcing children to give up something they may not be done playing with yet!

BUT Kristen, if we let a child play with something as long as they want, they will keep the toy all day and that isn't fair to other children.

They might. Children aren't used to having the power and control that can accompany keeping an item or toy for as long as they need it. They may enjoy this newfound power and exercise the control they are given. And that is OK!

Here are some things you can do to allow that child to exercise their power and help the waiting child.

◆ Start a waiting list. I had many clipboards stocked with paper and small golf pencils readily available in every area of the classroom. I encouraged children to write their names on a list so they would know that either I or the child with the coveted item would let them know when it's their turn. This is also really great name writing practice. Even if they can't write their name yet, I encourage some sort of mark or even the first letter of their name.

◆ If something is very popular, try to have more than one or even a few of that item. It could help alleviate long wait times.

◆ Empathize with the waiting child: "It is so hard to wait! What would you like to do while you wait?" or, "They may need to play with that shovel for a long time, would you like to swing or play in the mud kitchen while you wait?"

◆ Encourage the waiting child to problem-solve or use divergent thinking skills if the situation/item could have a substitution. "I wonder if you could find something that could scoop the sand kind of like that shovel?"

BUT Kristen, some children just hoard toys and won't let anyone else play with ALL of the horses. What do we do then?

This will absolutely happen. And our adult goggles can feel the unfairness in this and it can make us uncomfortable. We empathize with the waiting child because the child with ALL of the horses is really not thinking about others at this moment (and that is developmentally appropriate). In times like this, you can model empathy and problem-solving with the children.

Here are some things you can do:

◆ Empathize with the waiting child and suggest words they could say to the child with all the horses. "You want to play with some of the horses and Lo has them all. That is hard when someone has something you want. You could ask Lo for some of the horses."

  ◆ Lo says "No." I used to say something like this. "Lo, it looks like you have ALL the horses. Lottie is wondering if they can play with a couple of them. Can you let Lottie know when you are done with some of them so they can have a turn?" I have seen children hand over a few horses a few minutes later. They really just want it on their own terms!

◆ Try to find something similar for the waiting child. "I used to use blocks as horses when I was younger. Can I show you how I pretended blocks were horses when I was your age?"

◆ Get out the waiting list again, but this time have the child write a number (or dots or marks) next to their name to show how many horses they are waiting for (sneaking in some math concepts here). Tell the child with all the horses, "Lo is waiting for three horses, can you let her know when you are done with three of them?" Chances are the child may just be done with three horses in a few minutes! And if not, that is OK too.

BUT Kristen, sometimes a child might gather all the horses into the grocery cart and push them around, claiming they're playing with them even if they're not actively engaged with the toys.

To the adult eye, it may look like they aren't playing with the items in the grocery cart; but to the child pushing them around, they are most definitely playing with every single thing in that cart. Children engage in schema play in early childhood. Play schemas are patterns in children's play. One of the schemas children play around with is called transporting schema. The child moves items from one place to another. The items they are transporting are *all* involved in their play. They may also be engaging in the "filling and emptying" schema. It is just as it sounds, they like to fill and/or empty materials in the classroom! They filled up the grocery cart and then enjoyed transporting their materials around!

Reference

Shumaker, H. (2012). *It's OK Not to Share*. TarcherPerigee; Penguin.

A Letter to YOU

Dear Reader,

Years ago, I came upon the song "The Cape" by Guy Clarke and instantly felt connected to the lyrics. It describes the life of a person from childhood to old age and the risks they took, always trusting their cape when they needed it the most.

I have trusted my cape. And done some pretty epic things. But, the cape song is not about me. It is about you. It is about the children we serve. It is about your wild, play advocate heart that yearns to be free. It is the wild inside of each of you ready to be heard. It is the hero that will stand up for my child, your child and everyone's child. The hero that will fight for their right to a childhood filled with wonder, discovery, inquiry, play, and total cape magic.

The children that attend Butterfly Hill receive a special flour sack cape when they leave to head off to the world outside our magical yard. We put on our own adult capes alongside them, and we trust that there will be other adults that will fight for these children to live the childhood they are meant to live. We know we have given them the most developmentally appropriate childhood we could have. We know that they have been able to be children. Live into their full being. Live into their full creativity. Live into their whole purpose. We play "The Cape" song. We cry.

As early childhood educators, we are generally the last place these children get to live this life full of play, discovery, and wonder. I am asking you today: Can you please look after their childhood? Can you set your own wild heart free and advocate for them? I am passing my cape to you. Please trust it. The children are counting on you.

Always Trust Your Cape,
Kristen